Why Is Your Best Friend Your Best Friend?

75 Short Essays... And The Questions That Inspired Them

Edited by Al Desetta

True Stories by Teens

Why Is Your Best Friend Your Best Friend?

EXECUTIVE EDITORS
Keith Hefner and Laura Longhine

CONTRIBUTING EDITORS
Kendra Hurley, Nora McCarthy,
Sheila Feeney, and Rachel Blustain

LAYOUT & DESIGN
Efrain Reyes, Jr. and Jeff Faerber

COVER ART
YC Art Dept.

Copyright © 2009 by Youth Communication®

All rights reserved under International and Pan-American Copyright Conventions. Unless otherwise noted, no part of this book may be reproduced, stored in a retrieval system, or transmitted in any form or by any means, electronic, mechanical, photocopying, recording, or otherwise, without express written permission of the publisher, except for brief quotations or critical reviews.

For reprint information, please contact Youth Communication.

ISBN 978-0-9661256-7-2

Second Edition

Printed in the United States of America

Youth Communication®
New York, New York
www.youthcomm.org

Catalog Item #CW-WRIT-0

To the 25,000 teens who have
written essays for the
Youth Communication writing contests.

To the writers: We're honored to publish the essays in this book and thank our readers for submitting them. The opinions expressed in these essays are solely those of the authors. We were able to produce this book thanks to the generosity of an anonymous donor who is committed to making young people's voices heard. The proceeds from the sale of this book, if any, will go to help fund the Youth Communication teen writing program and prizes for teens in future essay contests. We lost contact with these writers long ago, but if you happen to be one of them, please notify us and we will send you two free copies of this book. If for some reason you do not want your essay published in a future edition, please contact us and we will remove it.

Table of Contents

11 **Introduction**

13 **How and Where to Use This Book**

WRITING PROMPTS ABOUT PEOPLE

31 Why Is Your Best Friend Your Best Friend?

32 How Would You Describe Your Family?

35 Write a Valentine to That Special Someone

36 Who Do You Trust?

37 Describe Your Ideal Mate

39 If One or Both of Your Parents Deserted You and Then Came Back Years Later Wanting to Know You, How Would You Handle It?

41 Who Are Better—Men or Women?

43 If You Could Give Your Teachers Grades. . .

45 Would You Go Out With Someone Who's Handicapped?

46 What Stereotypes Do You Think People Have of You That You Would Like to Change? Why?

47 If You Could Change Your Race, Would You?

49 Have You Ever Cheated on Your Boyfriend or Girlfriend?

51 What Makes You Angry? And What Do You Do About It?

53 If You Could Rid Yourself of Any Emotion, What Would It Be and Why?

55 Who's Your Most Memorable Teacher? Why Does He or She Stand Out?

Contents

- 57 If You Could Switch Places with Anyone, Who Would it Be?
- 59 Have You Ever Betrayed or Been Betrayed by a Friend? Explain.
- 61 Who Are You More Comfortable With— Your Friends or Your Family? Explain.

WRITING PROMPTS ABOUT IMPORTANT LIFE EVENTS

- 65 Describe Your First Love
- 66 What's the Greatest Natural High You've Ever Experienced?
- 68 What's the Scariest Thing that Ever Happened to You?
- 70 Love or Money?
- 72 Bad Hair Days
- 74 Describe Something One of Your Teachers Has Done That's Had a Big Effect on You
- 76 What's the One Thing You've Done in Your Life That You're Most Proud of and Why?
- 77 What's the Most Unusual or Dramatic Thing You've Done (or Can Imagine Doing) to Convince Someone to Go Out with You?
- 79 When Was the Last Time You Cried and Why?
- 81 How Was Your First Kiss, or How Would You Want It to Be?
- 82 What Is Your Biggest Regret?
- 84 If You Were to Die Today, What Would Your Friends and Family Say About You at Your Funeral?
- 86 What Is the Most Embarrassing Thing You've Ever Done and Why?

Contents

87   What Song or Movie Best Reflects Your Life, and Why?

89   What is the Most Spiteful Thing You've Done or Had Done to You? How Did It Make You Feel, and Why?

91   What's the Hardest Thing You've Ever Had to Do? Explain.

94   Describe Your Best or Worst Holiday Memory

96   What Would a Movie of Your Life Be About, and Who Would Play You?

99   What's a Mistake That You've Made That You Don't Regret? Explain.

102   What's Something You Hide From People That You Secretly Want Them to Know? Explain.

104   What's Your Most Memorable Summer Experience?

106   If You Could Go Back in Time and Change an Event In Your Life, What Would It Be? Why?

108   What Is the Funniest Thing That's Ever Happened to You?

110   Write a Letter to Your Parents, Telling Them What's Going On in Your Life That They Should Know About—but Don't

WRITING PROMPTS ABOUT SOCIAL ISSUES

113   What Does the American Flag Mean to You?

114   If You Could Bring Back a Dead Celebrity, Who Would It Be?

115   If You Could Solve One Problem Facing Teenagers, What Would It Be and How Would You Solve It?

Contents

116 What Should Teens Know or Do Before Having Sex?

118 Should Marijuana Be Legalized?

IMAGINATIVE WRITING PROMPTS

123 If You Had Supernatural Powers, What Would You Do?

124 What Happens After We Die?

125 How Is the World Going to End?

128 What Was the Weirdest Dream You Ever Had?

130 Say It in Slang: If I Ruled the World…:

131 What Brings Out the Beast in You?

133 If You Could Be Anybody in the World, Who Would You Be?

135 If You Had $10,000 and Only a Day to Spend It, What Would You Spend It On?

137 How Would It Feel to Be Your Favorite Color?

138 Describe the Night Time Through the Eyes of a 5-Year-Old

140 If You Could Have Someone Be Your Personal Slave for a Day, Who Would It Be?

141 A Double Life?

143 Your Own Words?

144 If You Could Adopt a Wild Animal, What Would It Be?

145 What Would You Do if You Only Had a Month to Live?

146 If the World Were to End Tomorrow, What Would You Miss the Most?

148 If You Could Be Anything in the World Besides a Human, What Would You Be? Why?

Contents

149   What Will Your Town or City Be Like in 50 Years?

150   What's One Change You Would Like to See in the Next Decade?

152   If You Could Be a Member of the Opposite Sex for One Day, What Would You Do? Why?

154   If You Could Have any Super Power, What Would It Be and Why?

156   If You Could Direct a Music Video, What Would It Be Like? What Would You Put in It? Why?

158   If You Could Create an Invention to Help Humanity, What Would It Be and What Would It Do?

160   If I Ruled the World...

162   What Place and Time Would You Travel Back To? Why?

164   What Would You Do If You Could Make Yourself Invisible?

167   If You Could Live in a Book, Movie, or TV Show, What Would It Be and Why?

169   If You Could Invent Something, What Would It Be? How Would It Work?

173   **Guide to Essays (Index) By Topic/Theme**

176   **By Genre/Style**

177   **About Youth Communication**

181   **About the Editor**

Introduction

Why Is Your Best Friend Your Best Friend? collects 75 essays by teens, submitted to writing contests that appear in *New Youth Connections*, a magazine by and for young people. *New Youth Connections* is published by Youth Communication, a non-profit writing and journalism program. The writing contest is one of the magazine's most popular features, attracting more than 25,000 entries since its inception in 1981. The essays in this collection, which address a wide range of topics and display great energy and imagination, are designed to help your students become more excited about and proficient in their own writing.

Writing has become an increasingly important skill for students to learn. The Scholastic Aptitude Test (SAT) now includes a writing section because it is an essential skill for success in college. And employers consistently report that good writing is one of the most important skills they look for in evaluating candidates for hiring and promotion.

Writing in response to a powerful prompt is also a wonderful way to get young people thinking about important issues in their lives—who they are, their relationships with family and friends, and who they want to become.

This book can help you make writing more interesting, particularly for students who are weak or reluctant writers. Young people often aren't motivated by standard writing assignments. Because these prompts were created by the teen staff of *New Youth Connections* to interest their peers and encourage entries, they are fresh and relevant and are much more likely to engage the interest of the young people in your classes.

Most importantly, the collected essays provide teens with tangible examples of successful writing by their peers, nearly all of whom attend public schools and, in some cases, are enrolled in remedial programs, ESL classes, GED prep classes, or other alternative settings. *Why Is Your Best Friend Your Best Friend?* offers a realistic selection of writing by teens of average ability and varied backgrounds who were inspired by good prompts to write with greater passion and precision. When young people see teens much like themselves writing successfully, it will give them the confidence that they can do so, too.

> **For Teachers:**

How and Where to Use This Book

There are two main uses for the prompts in this book: 1) To help teens improve their writing, and 2) To help teens think more deeply about their feelings, relationships, behavior, and goals. For example, if your goal is to help students improve their writing, you can use the prompts in these ways:

- ▶ As catalysts for the 5-paragraph essay, persuasive essays, descriptive writing, biographical writing, humorous essays. and other forms.

- ▶ As warm-up exercises before a longer writing assignment or class project.

- ▶ As practice for standardized writing tests.

If your goal is social and emotional learning, you can use the prompts in these ways:

- ▶ As a read-aloud to prompt discussion about how young people struggle with challenges similar to the ones that your students confront.

How to Use This Book

- ▶ As a pre-write, to help students think more deeply and to focus discussion.
- ▶ As a way for students to explore specific issues that the essays address, such as father/daughter relations, domestic violence, loss, and others (see the index, p. 175, for a list of topics covered in the stories).

If you're using these essays to help students think about social and emotional issues, they are doing double duty because the students are simultaneously practicing their reading and writing skills while they explore the issues.

How the Essays Are Organized

The essays in this book are grouped into four categories:

- ▶ Essays about people. For example, "How would you describe your family?"

- ▶ Essays about important life events. ("What's the greatest natural high you've ever experienced?")

- ▶ Essays about social issues. ("If you could solve one problem facing teenagers, what would it be and how would you solve it?")

- ▶ Imaginative essays. ("If you had supernatural powers, what would you do?")

These categories are somewhat arbitrary: an essay about an important life event usually involves people, and all the essays show imaginative thinking. But we've chosen these general categories to help you locate prompts that best suit your needs and interests, and those of your group. (For a list of stories by topic, from African-American Youth to Violence, see the index on page 175.)

How to Use This Book

Use the Essays to Teach Various Writing Styles and Forms

The essays display a wide variety of writing styles and can be used as examples of forms typically taught in secondary school, such as a portrait of a person, a description of a place, a persuasive essay, a compare and contrast essay, and many others. If you regularly teach these forms, you'll recognize them among the essays. We've highlighted excerpts from a few of those styles below, so you can offer students different ways to write about a topic. This will not only help you teach a variety of writing styles, but can also help students get "unstuck" if they have trouble getting started.

1) Description of a person

For students who are weak or reluctant writers, describing a person close to them can help them get started. They are already "experts" on the topic, so they can move right to focusing on the writing. With a little prompting and a good model like the one below, they are usually able to describe that person with a fair amount of physical and emotional detail. See how Saraya uses that detail to create a portrait of her dream boyfriend.

> PROMPT: DESCRIBE YOUR IDEAL MATE
>
> "PRICELESS..."
>
> My ideal mate would be cute. He'd have gorgeous milk chocolate eyes through which you could read the secrets of his soul. He would have a noble nose and full, kissable lips, and white teeth. He would not be too tall, but no shorter than me. He would be firm and lithe and warm. Yet, he would not be perfect. He would have his share of bumps and gross habits just like me.
>
> He would be quick-witted and intelligent. He would be both a leader and a follower, but always

master of his fate. His shoulders would be wide and strong to bear the burdens that life may ask him to carry. However, he would be wise enough to know when that load was too heavy and he would be unafraid to say, "I can't carry this any longer."

He would look to me as an equal in some things, yet not all. He would respect me as a human and treasure me as a woman. He would be unafraid to challenge my differences and yet he would always respect my right to be different. He would talk to me about what stirs his soul and lifts his spirit, what kindles his passions and ignites his anger, where and what he was in the past and where and what he will be in the future.

—SARAYA JAMES

2) Autobiography

Most of the writing prompts will encourage students to draw on personal experience as they write their responses. Personal experience offers a range of rich opportunities for young writers. Encourage them to look at their own lives in responding to the prompts, as Abu does below. (Note: Some students may feel that their experiences are not dramatic enough to warrant a story. Explain that the way they *tell* the story and their reflection on the experience are more important than the experience itself.)

> **PROMPT: WHAT'S THE HARDEST THING YOU'VE EVER HAD TO DO?**

Learning English

The hardest thing I've ever had to do was to learn English. When I came to America 11 years ago, I was 7 and in the 3rd grade. Even though I hated school because I didn't know how to speak English, I still had to go every day.

In the first two months my classmates came up to me and asked me questions, like "What's your name?" or "Where you from?" But I didn't know what they were asking me. I just stood there looking at them, like an idiot.

Meanwhile, I was always very quiet in class. But the kids tried to teach me curse words to say in front of the teacher or to other kids.

I was also scared to go to my gym class because sometimes the gym teacher asked all the students to get into groups. "We don't want you in our group," everyone hollered at me when I went up to them. Even though I didn't understand the language, I still knew by their facial expressions that I wasn't welcome in their group. I didn't know what to do, and didn't understand the games.

—Abu Nazakat

3) Humor

Encourage your students to use humor in their essays. Finding what's funny in a situation can lead to energetic writing.

> **Prompt: Bad hair days—Describe the worst experience you've had at the barber or hair stylist**
>
> A Bald Chia Pet
>
> As she massaged the relaxer cream into my hair, the stylist asked me had I ever had a perm. I said no, so she said she was only gonna leave it

on for 15 minutes. Within the first five minutes my scalp felt like it was on fire, but I didn't say anything because I figured it was supposed to do that. By the time 15 minutes passed I thought I was gonna die, not to mention that I thought I heard sizzling noises coming from my dome.

When she rinsed my hair out, she said, "Oh my God!" as clumps of my hair came out in her hands. I screamed and looked in the mirror. I had patches of hair missing everywhere. She said I had a chemical reaction to the lye. I started crying and she said with a few treatments, everything would be fine. She did what was left of my hair in a wrap, and I left looking like a bald chia pet.

No doubt it wasn't my man's best birthday, because instead of looking like the bomb, I looked like a bomb hit me! I look back and cry because I still have the scabs to remind me of the horror!

—CHRISTINA MARIE LOPEZ

4) Poetry

Most of the prompts can be answered in verse—which can take the form of traditional poetry, free verse, hip-hop, or anything in between. Look at how Joseph responded in verse to the following prompt.

PROMPT: DESCRIBE THE NIGHT TIME THROUGH THE EYES OF A 5-YEAR-OLD

GOOD NIGHT? YEAH, RIGHT!

Crack! Now what was that?
Was it someone's tire going flat?
Or was it a big green alien?

Strange Martian men
Coming with their big ray gun?
Will they force us to work on the sun?

Dumf! What was it now?
It's coming closer to the bed's bow!
It's too dark to see!
Is someone trying to get me?

AHHH! It just started to attack.
What to do now, should I just sit back?
I really wish I had my bat
To use against this giant green alien... Cat?

Phew, it's just a harmless feline.
I calmed down and now I'm fine.
I put down my pet,
Turned off the TV, and I was set.

Good night to all, good night to dad,
Good night to mom, I'm tired and I'm glad,
Good night to my cat Fred,
Most of all good night to the monster
under my bed!

—Joseph DiBiasi

5) Slang and dialect

Many young people are comfortable with slang and other non-traditional forms of language. In this example, the writer uses Jamaican patois to respond to a prompt that specifically asks for slang, but you can encourage writers to experiment with language for any of the prompts. Remind them, however, that slang has rules of usage which they need to follow. Whatever style they choose—slacker, metalhead, Valley Girl, Spanglish, black English, or a patois like the example below—it should be written so that a skilled speaker of that style would agree that it was accurate and authentic. For example, black English uses the "to be" construction differently than standard English, but the rules for using it are still strict. This is a harder lesson than most students think, and it can be a great opportunity to help students better understand the rules of standard English by comparing them with nonstandard forms. It is also an opportunity to acknowledge the value of students' home languages and dialects, which are different than, but not inferior to, standard English.

> **PROMPT: SAY IT IN SLANG: IF I RULED THE WORLD...**
>
> MI PUT DE CHIRAN FIRST
>
> Ef mi was de 'oman who ruled de world, mi tink 'ould stress more tings un ed-u-ca-tion. First of all, de chiran 'ould all wear uniforms. Fom de first standud tu de 12 stanud. De chiran ed-u-ca-tion 'ould be de success to mi country. De teachin' of chiran 'ould begin learning' fom de age of one. Dis a show de chiran values an give dem a positive feelin' towads de futua. Dey will use dis knowledge, dat 'av bin planted, since dey small tu ovacum world problems: pollution, poverty, an 'omlessness. Dis is 'ow mi a rule mi world. "De chiran is de future."
>
> —MARCIA BENONS STOUTE

6) Simile

A simile is a figure of speech in which one thing is likened to another thing to which it is not similar. In this case, Deeandra imagines herself to be the wind. Encourage your students to use similar imaginative devices in responding to the prompts.

> **PROMPT: IF YOU COULD BE ANYTHING IN THE WORLD BESIDES A HUMAN, WHAT WOULD YOU BE? WHY?**
>
> THE WIND
>
> If I could be anything in the world, I'd want to be the wind. I would like to be the wind because I would be my own boss, blowing any way I feel like.
>
> When I'm mad, I could spin fast to make a tornado, so that the world would know my rage. And on a hot summer day, I could blow a cool breeze, so I could watch kids come out and frolic.
>
> I could bring lost loves back together, or choose to blow victim and murderer apart. I couldn't change minds but I could change lives. I could blow so cold, one could freeze to death. Or stop blowing, so windmills couldn't work and farmers couldn't water their crops—nothing could grow and everyone would die.
>
> If I'm the wind, I'll have the power to create, destroy, and illuminate.
>
> —DEEANDRA LEESHUE

7) Dialogue

Dialogue can be another way of inspiring weak or reluctant writers—it can be relatively easy as well as fun to write, and some prompts can be answered almost entirely in dialogue. See how Channell uses dialogue in her essay.

> **PROMPT: IF YOU WERE TO DIE TODAY, WHAT WOULD YOUR FRIENDS AND FAMILY SAY ABOUT YOU AT YOUR FUNERAL?**
>
> 'SHE FELT BEST WHEN SHE SAW OTHER PEOPLE HAPPY'

"Um, Mrs. Brooks, we have to bring the coffin out," says the funeral director.

"Okay, can you give me one more minute?"

"Yes."

The funeral director leaves and my mom continues to stare at me. She fixes my hair a little and says, "I always thought it was going to be the other way around. Many parents never let the thought of their children dying before them surface in their minds. I will never forget you no matter how old I get, and I will always love you."

She kisses my forehead and walks away. I love you too, mom.

As I watch my coffin being pushed out to where all the guests are, I really start to think about how I'm going to miss everyone, but in the end—not to be all morbid—I'm sure I will be able to see them and speak to them again.

The funeral starts.

My dad speaks: "I'm not one who usually shows my emotions, but today I can't hold them in. She was my first child and her mom and I separated when she was 3. Even though she had problems with depression, I hoped that since we were both there for her she would be all right. But I feel I should have showed a little more love. She would always try to give me a hug and I would always push her away. I never really told her that I loved her, so I would like to take this opportunity to say something to her because I know she can hear me...I love you, Channell."

My friend Kathleen speaks: "I will be speaking on behalf of all of Channell's friends. She was the nicest, most caring and honest friend that we have ever had. Channell always kept us laughing even when a situation wasn't all that funny. She once told me that she felt best when she saw other people happy and enjoying themselves. That's where she got her joy from."

—Channell Brooks

78) The letter

For many students, the letter is a familiar and comfortable form. It can give a focus to their thoughts and emotions. The following prompt specifically asks for a response in letter form, but students can use that form to answer many of the prompts.

> **Prompt: Write a letter to your parents telling them what's going on in your life that they should know about—but don't**
>
> Dear Mom and Dad,
>
> First of all, I want to tell you guys that I love you very much and that I think that you guys have done a great job raising me. But I think that it's time to let me go.
>
> You guys know that I'm 16 years old, a senior, president of the National Honor Society, and my grades are in the top of my class. But I guess you aren't satisfied with that, because you're always thinking that I'm going to do something wrong, when I don't even have a boyfriend.
>
> I want you to know that there is this guy that I really like, and if he asks me out I'm going to say yes, even though I know that if you guys find out, you're both going to have heart attacks. I'm sorry, but I'm tired of boredom in my life. I want to be

free.

You guys think that by treating me like a little kid and not letting me hang out with my friends, you are doing me a favor, but I don't think so. Sometimes I feel worthless, like I'm alone in this world. That's because you treat me like I'm handicapped. Please let me live my life. I promise you I won't disappoint you.

I love you both very much.

—Elena

9) Comparison

Ask students to compare or contrast two differing ideas, points of view, experiences, etc. In this case, to debate who's the better sex Tisha pretends she is a man.

Prompt: Who are better—men or women?

Big Egos v. Big Hearts

Although I am of the female gender, I have decided to look at this issue through a male's eyes. Are men better because we hold great strength in many areas or are women better because they are blessed with the gift to give life?

It all comes down to one thing: We are all equal, and we all need one another. The only element that can bond us together is love. Unfortunately, men do not know how to love as well as women. That's what makes women superior in my eyes. It is not that men do not want to give love back. We just do not know how.

From the time I was produced from my mother's womb, I was taught to act like a man. To cry was demeaning and to be insensitive was acceptable. I had to project a tough exterior that was supposed to protect me from all pain.

How to Use This Book

> When the young lady I adored walked out of my life, God knows how badly I wanted to cry. I wanted to beg her to come back and try to work things out. To my father and friends, if I had taken those actions, I would not have been considered a man. It's times like that when a man is torn between his feelings and his image.
>
> Being hung up with an ego, a man is most likely to ignore his feelings. I often envy women for their openness in expressing their emotions. There are times when I wish I, too, could be like them.
>
> —Tisha Williams

10) Persuasive essay

Ask students to argue a specific point of view in their essays—such as whether the Pledge of Allegiance should be required, whether gun control violates the Second Amendment, or whether school uniforms are the answer to better discipline. In this case, Lina has never used marijuana, but argues for its legalization

> PROMPT: SHOULD MARIJUANA BE LEGALIZED?
>
> I have not once been tempted into using marijuana or any other illegal substance and am a 100% supporter of all efforts aimed to help and educate teenagers in the battle against drugs. But unfortunately, with each passing day, it appears to be a battle that can't be won.
>
> Use of marijuana has become a fact. Anti-drug abuse organizations set up for the benefit of troubled teens have been unsuccessful in destroying their curiosity and interest in marijuana.
>
> Past events support my statement. Prohibition, from 1919 to 1933, proved unsuccessful, as

gangsters like Al Capone emerged and bootleggers found ways to smuggle alcohol, despite the government's earnest attempts to stop them. As a result, the use of alcohol was legalized, since the attempt to make a "dry America" had sorely failed.

Despite the hazardous impact of marijuana, alcohol, cigarettes, and other such substances, laws that forbid their use are powerless to stop addicts. It is proven time after time that laws are constantly broken and that no law can be fully enforced on the public. Drug users will always find new ways of selling and using marijuana, despite the laws that forbid them to do so.

If marijuana is legally sold in pharmacies or hospitals, abuse of the substance could be spotted at an early stage. Common misconceptions and questions can be cleared up by professionals selling marijuana. They can ensure that the substance is authentic and will not cause damage to the user.

Legalizing marijuana is a drastic resort, but it may be worthwhile in the end if we manage to control the problem, rather than spend energy (in vain) in trying to completely abate it.

—Lina Georgieva

More Tips on Using the Writing Prompts

Each prompt is self-explanatory, asking students to write about a specific topic. In some cases there are follow-up questions to clarify or amplify the initial prompt. Use these follow-ups to encourage students who are reluctant writers or who have trouble getting started.

There are probably as many ways to use these prompts as there are teachers. We encourage you to adapt them to your style, the skills and needs of your students, and the requirements of your school or program.

Here are some suggestions for using the prompts.

▶ Tell students they will be doing a short writing assignment in response to a prompt that was created by another teen.

▶ If you plan to have students rewrite the piece, or if the writing will be used only to warm up for a discussion, you can tell them not to worry in their first draft about length or perfect spelling and grammar. The goal at this stage is to get students thinking.

However, if this will be the only draft students write, let them know the standards you expect them to strive for.

▶ Read aloud the writing prompt, and also write it on the board or chart paper. Ask students to think for a moment about how they might respond to the prompt. Then ask a few students to volunteer a couple of ideas.

▶ Tell the students you have an essay written by another teen in response to the prompt. Ask students to turn to that page in the book, or pass out a copy, and ask volunteers to take turns reading it aloud. While they're listening, ask students to underline words or passages they like or that stand out for them. The point of having them read a model essay is to help them identify examples they can use in their own essays. However, students will need help pinpointing the elements that make the model essay effective. Guide them in identifying these techniques, such as a catchy first line, good description, apt word choice, or a strong conclusion. Remind your students that they can adapt techniques used by the writer for their own essays. (At the same time, remind the group that the model essay is only one example of how the writing prompt can be answered. Students are free to develop their own responses.)

Note: If you have a specific objective in mind, such as helping students to improve the five-paragraph essay, or to write more descriptively, or to use correct spelling, be sure to give them clear instructions about what you expect so they will know what to aim for. And, of course, if this exercise is practice for a standardized test, modify your instructions to match the instructions students will get when they take the test.

▶ Read the writing prompt aloud a second time and ask students to start writing. Give them a specific amount of time to complete their essays. If the writing is merely a prompt for discussion, three minutes may suffice. For other purposes, you may allow as long as a whole class period.

▶ Volunteers can read aloud their finished (or draft) essays. Remind students of some of the elements they liked in the model essay, and ask them to point out where their peers have successfully incorporated those elements. Students love this kind of positive feedback. It's also good reinforcement. When they see that they've been able to recognize a technique in something they've read and use it themselves, it encourages them to do closer reading in the future. That's an important foundation for improving their writing.

Writing Prompts About People

> **PROMPT**
>
> Why Is Your Best Friend Your Best Friend?

She's Not Superwoman but...

Tina Li

No, she did not run into a burning building or stand in front of a speeding bullet to save my life, but what she does makes her every bit as valuable to me as a best friend. Just by her being there, I have found a confidante, a person to share joys and sorrows with, a person to have fun with, and just to talk to and be close to. She's one of the most sympathetic and understanding people I know and I don't know of anyone who is as willing as she is to share in my burdens.

In junior high, when my other friends used to tease me, she would come to my defense when my feelings were hurt. When this bully used to pull my hair, she would step in and say, "She's sensitive; pull mine instead." These little things add up to make her a wonderful and caring friend.

She always reminds me to call her if I have any problems with school or my family, telling me no matter how busy she is she will squeeze in a couple of minutes to listen. She even offered to accompany me to the hospital after school when I had to go to check some personal problems.

I can always count on her to have a good time and to make me feel better when I'm down. She's a lot of fun to be with, has a great sense of humor, is witty and intelligent, and possesses just about all the qualities that make a best friend. We go to different high schools now, but we still keep in touch by phone. I may not see her every day, but I know she will always be one of the best friends I'll ever have. ■

PROMPT

How Would You Describe Your Family?

Write an essay telling a friend from another country what they would have to know to feel comfortable visiting your home and living with your family.

For example:

—What foods do you eat?
—What is your religion (and is it important to you)?
—What music do you listen to?
—How do you like to 'keep' your house?
—Who does the chores?
—What TV shows do you watch?
—What activities are encouraged in your home (games, talking, reading, dancing, dating, etc.), and what activities are forbidden?
—Who has final authority?

Welcome to My Family

Latrina Neal

My name is Latrina Neal. My family and I are glad you are coming to visit our home. I know you are going to enjoy it here, but first I am going to give you some information about my family that will make you feel more comfortable visiting my home and living with my family.

There are a few people that you will get to know. First is my mother. She is a nice, Christian, church-going woman. She gives respect and only asks that you give respect in return. She loves kids who take an interest in religion and music.

My religion is Pentecostal. In this religion we believe there is only one God. We do not worship statues. We also believe in the Holy Trinity and the Ten Commandments. We say prayers regularly. My father is a minister. He is very loving and has faith in people and stands behind you to support and encourage you. He is respectable and believes in honesty.

My sister is 12. She is very outgoing and she will listen to your problems. She is very trustworthy and dependable. I think highly of her and I know you will too.

My brother is 16 and he is a typical teenager. He likes sports and he doesn't stay inside much. Sometimes he can be very understanding and kind, and sometimes...well, let's just say he could be called a free spirit and a pest.

I have a very big family and we all gather together to celebrate many events and holidays. They will all welcome you with open arms.

My parents listen to gospel music. It is inspiring and has much to do with religion. My brother likes rap which is what most typical teenagers around us listen to. I like soft rock. It is soothing and relaxing. I love the songs and usually record them.

We like to keep our house clean because my mother and father always say cleanliness is next to Godliness. We all share the work. My parents assign chores to do. My brother has to take out the trash and sweep and sometimes mop the floor. I wash dishes. My sister helps too. We all pitch in and help each other.

The one who has final authority in my house is usually my mother. If she approves sometimes you get to do it.

I watch TV a lot and play games like Monopoly, chess, checkers, Yahtzee, and video games.

We talk to each other and confide in each other about certain things. We are not afraid to express ourselves fully. We have a time in my house when the TV and the stereo and all other distracting things are put away and we just have quiet time. It is a time I use to study. My sister is more the dancer.

Why Is Your Best Friend Your Best Friend?

Because my father is a pastor we don't usually play music loud or dance a lot.

My parents say dating can start at age 16. They are old-fashioned and they think that a boy should meet the parents on the first date. He must be a Christian and have good manners and morals. The #1 activity that is forbidden in my house is lying. My parents believe in honesty and truth.

They expect us to obey the rules and regulations while living under their roof. They expect you to give respect. They want you to have a good time but also want you to be careful. To feel comfortable around my family you just have to be yourself and be courteous and respectful.

You will have to love children because you will be around lots of kids. You will have to be ambitious and have a goal in life, or something you want to achieve in the future. You must want to make something of yourself.

I know it would be hard to fit into each and every description of the family. No one is perfect and my family is not all that hard to get along with. All you need to know to visit us is our basic morals and values. I know you are going to have a good time with us. ■

Writing Prompts About People

> **PROMPT**
>
> ## Write a Valentine to That Special Someone
>
> What is it about them that drives you wild? Tell them what they mean to you, how they make you feel, and your secret plans for them.

Weak Kneed But Willing

Dana Johnson

My knees get weak
My tongue won't work
My laugh gets loud,
I feel like a jerk.
My palms sweat,
My mouth goes dry.
I ask myself,
Why him, WHY?

Is it your smile
Or your deep voice?
Whatever it is,
I have no choice.
You're in my mind
Morning to night
Whether in person
Or out of sight.
Anywhere I am,
You're with me
It's unbelievable
Don't you agree?

I see you now,
Your face is here.
Are you my soulmate?
If you are, my dear,
The time has come
To face the facts
We are a pair,
The perfect match.
Don't waste a moment,
There's none to spare.
I'm waiting for you.
Don't you care? ∎

WHY IS YOUR BEST FRIEND YOUR BEST FRIEND?

> **PROMPT**
> **Who Do You Trust?**
> —Why do you trust them? Why not?
> —What does it mean for someone to earn your trust. To betray it?

Friends? Father? Strangers? God?

Vuan Mae

On a dark, chilly night, a frail lady stumbles and falls onto the prickly ground. At the sight of this, a stranger rushes to her aid but walks away shuffling through her purse. Meanwhile, she lies on the street with bruises more severe than those inflicted by a fall.

A student tells her close girlfriend the darkest of secrets. Her friend solemnly promises not to reveal anything. Several days later, her secret becomes hallway gossip.

A father playfully tells his young child to leap from the dinner table, saying that he'll catch him in the air. The boy throws himself into his father's arms. He lands painfully on his face only to learn from his own father the consequences of trust.

An "A+" college undergraduate with a potentially prosperous future has repeatedly been taught the dangers of IV drug use. Nonetheless, the needle in his arm makes him feel euphoric, as he walks on the ledge of a six-story building.

The lady can't trust the stranger; the girl can't trust her friend; the boy can't trust his father; the drug addict can't trust himself.

Who do we trust? In God, we trust? Isn't it ironic that a phrase so sacred is printed on a bill so materialistic?

Thus, don't ask: "Who do you trust?" Ask "Who CAN you trust?" And the answer: no one. ■

Writing Prompts About People

PROMPT

Describe Your Ideal Mate

Not Perfect, But Priceless

Saraya James

I knew him once...the perfect man. We met on a beautiful summer day. He was my Arabic teacher. I walked into the classroom, small, hot and crowded, and there he was—the man of my dreams... Taariq.

He was gowned in flowing white robes and his voice was like the rolling waves of the Pacific. Short yet tall, he commanded respect with a glance. With a look he could capture hearts; he imprisoned mine.

It seems like yesterday. It was not. It was almost five years ago and I was just 11 years old. He was only 16.

My ideal mate would be cute. He'd have gorgeous milk chocolate eyes through which you could read the secrets of his soul. He would have a noble nose and full, kissable lips, and white teeth. He would not be too tall, but no shorter than me. He would be firm and lithe and warm. Yet, he would not be perfect. He would have his share of bumps and gross habits just like me.

With a glance he would draw me to him, where in his arms the troubles of my world would appear minuscule. With a touch he would be able to still the tidal waves in my heart. With a mere kiss he would bring to me exotic passions and an epiphany of the mysteries between man and his woman.

He would be quick-witted and intelligent. He would be both a leader and a follower, but always master of his fate. His shoulders would be wide and strong to bear the burdens that life may ask him to carry. However, he would be wise enough to know when that load was too heavy and he would be unafraid to say, "I can't carry this any longer."

He would look to me as an equal in some things, yet not all. He would respect me as a human and treasure me as a woman. He would be unafraid to challenge my differences and yet he would always respect my right to be different. He would talk to me about what stirs his soul and lifts his spirit, what kindles his passions and ignites his anger, where and what he was in the past and where and what he will be in the future.

He gave me all that I could want and he made me happy. He loved me and he liked me. He desired me and respected me. He gave to me the romance and passion that I craved. We were friends. We were lovers. We were brother and sister, husband and wife. In him I found strength and loyalty. In him I found true love...or so I thought.

Now I'm 16 and he's 21. We've both changed and yet we've remained the same. When we're together we no longer talk as much as we used to. The fierce passion we once shared has ebbed like the tide after a storm. The love, however, hasn't changed. He is no longer perfect in my eyes, for I have grown beyond the needs and desires, the dreams and fantasies, of a young girl.

I believe the perfect man will elude me forever. Yet experience has shown me I neither want or need the perfect man—for the one I have is priceless. ■

Writing Prompts About People

PROMPT

If One or Both of Your Parents Deserted You and Then Came Back Years Later Wanting to Know You, How Would You Handle It?

I'd Have Mixed Emotions

Cheryl Harmon

Being deserted by a parent is something that no child can ever forget. It is the saddest day of a young child's life, whether they know it or not. The only way to define how my mother deserted me is: coldly.

It was the week before Christmas and we had made the trip to grandma's house. I always went to my grandmother's house on weekends, but this weekend was different because my mother never came back for me.

I was about 5 at the time and I can only remember continually asking my grandmother why my mother had not come back yet. My grandmother would just say that my mother needed time to be alone and that she would come for me when she was ready. I never really knew what she meant by that but after asking for a while, I finally came to the conclusion that my mother didn't want me anymore and that she wasn't coming back.

So, as the years went on, I began to settle in well with my grandmother and my mother was never mentioned until a month before my junior high school graduation.

I had just gotten home from school and was surprised to see the sad look on my grandmother's face when I entered the room. She told me that my mother had just called and that she was on her way over to come and take me home.

I was overwhelmed with anger and sorrow. My mother was finally coming for me, but why did it take her so long? Nine years! Nine years is a long time! A very long time! Why did she call now? And why not earlier?

I was confused. And this confusion made me angry. I stormed out of the room and told my grandmother that I didn't want to see my mother and that I didn't want to go home with her! I hated her! I hated the fact that she disappeared from my life and was now trying to push her way back in.

When my mother came, I refused to see her. I remained in my room trying to figure out why she had come back for me. Did she finally miss me? Was she finally ready for me? Or did guilt send her back to me?

After several tears were shed, I decided to come out of my room and meet my mother.

She was not how I remembered her. She looked much older, more professional-like. She had a big smile on her face and hugged me as soon as I entered the room. There were tears in her eyes and she kept saying how much she missed me and how much she loved me. The coldness in my heart started to go away as she explained to me why she left and that she would never leave me again.

We soon developed the closeness that we have now, but deep down my grandmother will always be my real mother and I will never forget what being deserted feels like. ■

> **PROMPT**
> Who Are Better—Men or Women?

Big Egos v. Big Hearts

Tisha Williams

Although I am of the female gender, I have decided to look at this issue through a male's eyes. Are men better because we hold great strength in many areas or are women better because they are blessed with the gift to give life?

It all comes down to one thing: We are all equal, and we all need one another. The only element that can bond us together is love. Unfortunately, men do not know how to love as well as women. That's what makes women superior in my eyes. It is not that men do not want to give love back. We just do not know how.

From the time I was produced from my mother's womb, I was taught to act like a man. To cry was demeaning and to be insensitive was acceptable. I had to project a tough exterior that was supposed to protect me from all pain.

When the young lady I adored walked out of my life, God knows how badly I wanted to cry. I wanted to beg her to come back and try to work things out. To my father and friends, if I had taken those actions, I would not have been considered a man. It's times like that when a man is torn between his feelings and his image.

Being hung up with an ego, a man is most likely to ignore his feelings. I often envy women for their openness in expressing their emotions. There are times when I wish I, too, could be like them.

Women think it is easy to just walk away from them as they give life to your child. In fact it is quite difficult. Just because we are taught to act like "men" does not mean we were taught to be responsible. The fear of losing your freedom and becoming a father makes you run away. Even if you walk out of your child's life, that does not mean you forget about them. There are days you sit and think about what you have done. By the time you figure a way to fix your wrongdoing, it might be too late.

Committing to one person can also be scary. Women think men do not fear getting hurt, but we do. That is why some of us tend not to be faithful. We figure the more females you have a relationship with, the less chance of getting hurt. A man wants to love and be responsible; it is being frightened that makes him the opposite.

It is true that we can be egotistical, inconsiderate, irresponsible, selfish, and unfaithful. But there are good characteristics we possess as well. Many men will say men are better than women. Many women will say women are better than men. Between both sexes, love might be the only emotion we can agree upon. Most women have wonderful qualities that we men tend to take for granted. It's too bad we do not know how to appreciate them for that. ■

Writing Prompts About People

PROMPT

If You Could Give
Your Teachers Grades...

Gotta Have Heart and Humor

Michael Coderro

In grading teachers, the only fair way I can think to do it is by their teaching style. To actually go into their specific projects, individual idiosyncracies, hairdos or styles of dress would be too exhausting. Besides, they grade us on our academic and professional performances, so it's only fair we do the same.

I had to think up new and more specific letter grades for grading teachers. For instance, an "AAA" on a teacher's report card would designate them as "All-Around Awesome." These are those few but precious teachers we will never forget and wish there were more of. They plan interesting lessons. They have heart and dedication, but haven't left their sense of humor behind. These are the teachers whose classes you look forward to and enjoy putting in the extra effort because you know how often they do the same for you.

Another grade that might appear on a teacher's report card would be "DO" or "O": "Disorganized" or "Organized." This is a factor that is extremely important in how smoothly a class goes. Not only is it convenient and more efficient when the class organizer is organized, but there is nothing worse than knowing you did a good job on a report and earned a high grade, yet the teacher can't return it to you because she lost it.

The following grades can be used in the traditional style: "GA": "Gets Attention." A "GA-" might be received by someone like my economics teacher in junior high school. Her only attention-getting tactic was to drop a heavy book on the desk. A "GA+" could be earned by my former art or American history teachers. My art teacher is a funny guy who would get everyone's attention with his wit. My American history teacher was a very feisty guy who would start debates in order to get us into the class.

Another very important grade would be "GE": "Gives Encouragement." Teachers who earn a "GE+" are inches away from being a perfect teacher. Encouragement is such an important part of a student's self-confidence and motivation. This means that those teachers who recieve "GE-" have lots of work to do because to put down or discourage a student is the last thing that will ever propel them to do better.

I don't know if I feel completely comfortable naming specific names, but the teachers I've had should know what their report cards would look like. I'm just happy that I can honestly say that many more teachers would pass than fail. ∎

PROMPT

Would You Go Out With Someone Who's Handicapped? Why or Why Not?

Bigger Than the Insults

Robert Barber

I would go out with someone who's handicapped because you shouldn't judge someone because of their physical appearance. It's not about what they look like—it's about what's inside. He or she might be the sweetest person.

I've gone out with a girl who was handicapped and she was so nice to me. She only had one arm. My friend used to laugh and call her names but she was bigger than the insults and it didn't bother her. She just kept her head up, smiled, and kept on walking. I really liked her. She was sweet, caring, generous, and warm-hearted. We would still be going out if she hadn't moved.

I would go out with a handicapped person again. There are people in the world who act more handicapped than a handicapped person. So, people who say no to going out with a handicapped person should check themselves. ∎

PROMPT

What Stereotypes Do You Think People Have of You That You Would Like to Change? Why?

'I'll Be More Than a Gangbanger'

Jade Gardener

The stereotypes people have of me might outnumber the years that I have been alive. Because my neighborhood is violent, I imagine that people think I am a violent person, and because of the clothes I choose to wear, they might think I'm a gang member.

People probably stereotype me as a young girl from a broken home who will never come out to be anything except a drug dealer, drug addict, or gang member. They think I'll end up in jail or be on welfare with many kids. People probably think that if I wear expensive clothes that I stole the money to get them or sell drugs to get the money.

These stereotypes are horrible! I want the stereotypes people have of me and other minorities to change because youth are being told that they won't amount to anything and we grow up believing in failure. It breaks us down, then our neighborhood, and in turn our whole society. ∎

Writing Prompts About People

PROMPT

If You Could Change Your Race, Would You? Why or Why Not?

Rising Above the Past

Kirah Muhammad

I, in fact, am very proud to be an African-American. Yet, there was a time when I wanted, and actually tried, to change my race.

I was very young, about 3 or 4. One day, while walking with my mother, I passed by a white girl about the same age as I. I recall watching with envy the way her golden strands of hair flowed behind her like oceans of sunshine. I found myself reaching into my own hair: short, coarse, and bristly. Not at all flowing as the white girl's. I then become convinced that in order to have long soft hair, I would have to be white.

When I got home, I tried to make myself white. I took some white cream, maybe facial cream, and spread it all over my body and face. In my unripened mind, I figured if I let it stay on long enough it would seep through my skin and I'd turn white. So, I waited and waited. However, my wait was short-lived. As soon as my mother came in and saw me, she made me go to the tub and wash the stuff off.

Now, as I approach womanhood, my perspective on my black race has broadened. I went from resenting the traits given to me by my African ancestors to embracing and appreciating them. I've come to realize what being black is about. Black is beauty and strength. Black is rising above all that tries to keep one down—seeing through the prejudice, the unfounded hate, and the stereotypical misconceptions. There's so much history behind being black and I'm proud to be a part of it.

As for my hair, I am long beyond my shame. It's the crown piece of my African ancestry, and that is something for which I am filled with pride. ■

> **PROMPT**
>
> ## Have You Ever Cheated On Your Boyfriend or Girlfriend?
>
> Why or why not? If so, do you regret it now?

No Trust, No Relationship

Violet Chillous

To this question, my answer is "no." I have never cheated on any of my boyfriends and I don't plan to. I feel it's wrong and I wouldn't want it to be done to me. To cheat on my boyfriend would be the same as cheating myself and not being true to myself is the worst thing I can do. I always ask myself: What's the point of cheating on the one I'm with? Why would I even get involved and make that commitment if I was bound to break it? That would not just be wasting my time but his as well.

I would rather not make that commitment, so I could have the opportunity to do what I like, with whoever I want, without feeling guilty.

I know a lot of young couples that have problems and are on the verge of breaking up. And the main reason for this is suspicion of cheating or actually cheating. If I were them, I couldn't be in a relationship where I'd be wondering whether or not my man is cheating on me. That's where trust comes in. If there's no trust then there's no relationship.

I ask my friends who are guilty of cheating on their mates why they do it, and the most common explanation I've received is, "Well, he or she played me, so I'm gonna play him or her." When they tell me this I laugh in their faces. It seems to me that all they

Why Is Your Best Friend Your Best Friend?

want is the satisfaction of getting revenge. But why go through all that drama when you can get even more satisfaction when you're single like me? I'm able to do what I like with whoever and whenever. Cheating…what's the point? ■

PROMPT

What Makes You Angry? And What Do You Do About It?

No More Ignorance About Sex

Alexis Rojas

There are plenty of things that make me mad in this world, but the one thing that makes me especially upset is the fact that people get themselves involved with things they know little or nothing about. Like sex. So many people do it for so many reasons, but don't know the facts about it. I hear about so many people having sex and see so many young girls who end up with babies before they're ready that it upsets me. I wish people would take the time to know a little bit more before they go and do it.

That's not all that upsets me though. It also upsets me that not enough places are teaching people about sex. People do not like to talk about it and schools don't even want to teach it! It's as if people aren't supposed to be doing it, but a lot of us know that's not true. I've seen too many friends make mistakes in their lives when it comes to sex and that's why I am where I am right now.

One day while I was in the waiting room at the Mt. Sinai Adolescent Clinic, some young people came in with a TV. They showed a video on safe sex, spoke about it and answered questions, and then gave out condoms. Before they left, they mentioned that the program they were part of was hiring. I picked up an application on my way out. It was for a program called SPEEK (Sinai Peers Encouraging Empowerment through Knowledge), on the clinic's 2nd floor. I was called back for several interviews and after much waiting I was told that the job was mine. I had to go through rigorous training over the summer, which covered everything and anything about sex and relationships.

I am now an official peer educator at SPEEK. We go to lots of schools and plenty of other places educating kids mostly about safe sex, but we also do a lot of stuff on male/female anatomy and stuff like that. It makes me feel good to do what I do. I like knowing that I am making a difference and helping others make the right choices for themselves. When we go to places sometimes, the people know very little about what we're talking about, but when we leave they understand and know a whole lot more and it feels good to make an impact like that on someone. I like doing what I do because I know I am part of a solution and not a problem. ■

Writing Prompts About People

PROMPT

If You Could Rid Yourself Of Any Emotion, What Would it Be and Why?

Guilt Follows Me Like a Shadow

Carmen Munoz

If I could get rid of any emotion, it would be guilt. It follows me like a shadow and hovers over me as if I were its prey. I've become sick and tired of blaming myself for everything I did when my mother was alive. I often wish I could turn back the hands of time. The simple fact of not being able to say, "Sorry for all the pain I have caused you, Mom," haunts me day to day.

My mother and I were like sisters. We shared our deepest secrets with one another and trusted each other. This relationship sometimes caused us to fight but also brought us closer to each other. Even though my dad would see me on some weekends, my mother played the key role in my life.

I was very close to my mom when I was a child, but when I hit my early teens, that's where the trouble began. I was rebellious and disrespectful. I made my mother cry a lot, especially when I didn't get my way. I was selfish and inconsiderate. I acted cold-hearted towards her knowing she only had a few months to live. I didn't want to accept that my mother, the person I loved most, was going to die and I couldn't do anything to keep her alive.

My reaction towards her illness was denial. After I was aware that she was going to pass away, I was upset at the world and took my frustrations out on her. When she cried at night and went to the bathroom, puking her brains out, I yelled, "Shut up, Mom. I'm

Why Is Your Best Friend Your Best Friend?

trying to sleep." When she had breathing problems and began to turn blue, I just walked away and went downstairs to hang with my friends as if everything were normal.

When my mom was at the hospital, I refused to visit her. I went a couple of times, but didn't say much to her. I felt as if she was leaving me alone in this huge world. I was afraid to show what I was feeling. I was slowly breaking down inside. I never got to say goodbye to my mother because she passed away unexpectedly one December morning at 3:00 a.m. and that's where my guilt sits.

So now I have this guilt that I live with, a simple thing I could've resolved by just saying, "Sorry mother for all the pain I caused," and hearing her say, "I accept your apology." I would feel comfortable inside, instead of feeling a shadow chase me wherever I go. I feel as if guilt will follow me for the rest of my life on earth. ∎

Writing Prompts About People

> **PROMPT**
>
> Who's Your Most Memorable Teacher? Why Does He Or She Stand Out?

I Learned About Art —And About Myself

Helen Valencia

On the day in 8th grade we were forced to pick a talent, I made sure I didn't pick art. It wasn't that I didn't like it. I'd loved art since the 4th grade. I disregarded art this time for a very simple reason: She taught it.

Ms. Valentine was...oh, where to start...let's just say she was one of the most hated teachers in the 8th grade. She was demanding, tough, and loud.

And she didn't care about physical beauty. I never saw her with makeup on, while all the other female teachers struggled to match everything, from their shoes to their nail polish. Ms. Valentine seemed to struggle against color coordination, even though she was an art teacher. I remember one particular outfit she wore consisting of brown jeans and a green T-shirt, which hung loosely over her skinny body. As a self-conscious 8th grader, I winced when I saw her in that awful outfit.

Despite my efforts not to, I still ended up in Ms. Valentine's art class. She saw no one had sat down in her section of the auditorium (on the first day of the semester when we had to pick a talent class), so she walked around picking kids out of their chosen talents and putting them into her class. Since I had been in her 7th grade art class, Ms. Valentine spotted me through her large-framed glasses and marked me for entrapment.

But as the year passed by, I grew to admire this strange woman. Ms. Valentine truly loved art. It was a contagious passion and I opened my ears and started to really listen. How else would I have learned the significance of Picasso's masterpiece *Guernica*? I was hooked.

We painted, drew, and sculpted. One assignment, which involved papier-mache and other materials, consisted of making our own little sculpture. My sculpture was of a woman running, and I wanted her frozen in a natural running position.

Every time I thought I'd finished it, Ms. Valentine found something wrong with it and pointed it out, sending me back to my work table, frustrated. A couple of days later I really did finish it, and it turned out to look exceptionally good. That's when I realized this lady did know what she was talking about.

Over the months I became one of her favorite students and I even engaged in conversations with this unpopular teacher. I can remember her so clearly, putting up students' artwork, patches of sweat under her armpits. My first thought had been "disgusting," but then I realized her sweat was symbolic. It symbolized her passion for art. She loved it so much she didn't care much about anything else.

When I graduated junior high, I was satisfied with what I'd learned from her. I'd never known art was so beautiful and meaningful. Ms. Valentine taught me a lot about art and a little about life. At first, I didn't like her, but I grew to like her and, more importantly, respect her.

I still respect her because of who she is. She taught me not to be superficial and just be myself, to grow up and become who I want to be. If that's not memorable, I don't know what is. ■

Writing Prompts About People

> **PROMPT**
>
> If You Could Switch Places With Anyone, Who Would It Be, and Why?

I Want to Know Dad Better

Suejey Vasquez

My father and I don't get along. We both have very strong personalities and they clash. My father and I have never really had a conversation before; although we live in the same house, it's like we're strangers. So I want to switch places with my father because I want to understand him better as a person.

My father is a hard worker. He started off working as a clerk. He didn't make much money, so he was forced to take on another job as a landscaper. He kept looking for higher-paying jobs. My father didn't want to settle for a low-paying job. He knew he had a wife and four children at home who needed him. I admire that about my father—he never settled for anything and always had his eye on something higher.

But no matter how little money my father made, we always had enough. My father made sure my brothers, sisters, and I had enough food, clothes, and school supplies. He also made sure that all the bills were paid on time. I can't complain of ever not having enough, because ever since I can remember my father gave me everything.

Besides being a hard-worker, my father is also very heroic. He served eight years in the U.S. Army. I admire my father for serving our country for so many years, especially since he wasn't born in the U.S. Not many people would do that for a country that they weren't born in.

Although my father's been such a great person, I wish we had a better relationship. It's very hard to not get along with a person who's done so much for me. My father isn't very communicative with me, so I want to switch places with him because I want to understand who he really is. I want to know what he feels inside, and why it is that we can't get along.

There are a lot of people in this world who grow up without a father, and I, a person who's grown up with a hardworking father, can't even talk to mine. I think if I switched places with my father, our relationship would definitely improve.

I'd be able to understand how he feels being such a hard worker. It would be interesting to understand how my father feels about me, and why we can't get along. ■

Writing Prompts About People

PROMPT

Have You Ever Betrayed or Been Betrayed by a Friend? Explain.

I Spilled His Secret

Anonymous

When I betrayed my best friend, I felt horrible. Honestly, I didn't mean to do it. He told me something that he would rarely tell anyone. He even had friends he'd known since childhood and hadn't told them. He told me he was bisexual.

He was comfortable with himself but rarely trusted people enough to tell them about his bisexuality. When he told me, it was the first time that we'd ever really talked and gotten to know one another. I asked him if he was bisexual and he took a long time to answer the question. When that happened, I knew that he was. He finally did answer, "Yes." It was the start of a great friendship.

We became very close within weeks, sharing secrets about things that had happened when we were young. We hung out every day. We were very loyal to one another, even when that loyalty and trust was tested.

For instance, a guy in school told my best friend rumors that I was a messed-up friend to him and I was no good. We approached him and asked why he was doing that. When he stuttered trying to answer the question, my friend knew he was lying.

But a few months ago, I was talking to a girl and she asked me if my friend was bisexual. I didn't answer. Then we were talking about people being bisexual, wondering, "How are they attracted to the same gender?"

While talking, I accidentally said my friend was bisexual. I

Why Is Your Best Friend Your Best Friend?

thought to myself, "Damn, I screwed up." I told her not to tell anybody, but I had a feeling it was going to come back to me.

My friend found out and asked me why I'd betrayed him. I told him the truth and how it had happened, but he didn't believe me and said he didn't want to be friends anymore. I kept apologizing but he didn't want to hear it. That was the end of our friendship.

To this day, I still feel messed up about doing this. Every time I think about it, I wish I could relive that day and handle it the right way. I would trade everything I have in my life to be friends again. I hope he can forgive me one day. ■

PROMPT

Who Are You More Comfortable With—Your Friends or Your Family? Explain.

A Balancing Act

Mia Giardina

When I get together with family members whom I haven't seen in a year, I feel I need to put my best "face" on. I usually act very respectfully and rather quietly with my older family members. I feel more comfortable on a day to day basis with my friends, because I don't feel as if I need to present myself in any particular way.

This Passover, as my extended family gathered around the dinner table, everybody acted as they do every year on this holiday. My aunt told stories about her son's progress in school, his fight with a friend. My mother told everybody about her new job. People asked me what college I want to attend in the fall. On the whole, everything was the same as it had been the year before.

One factor was different, though. I had brought my best friend with me, who is Muslim and Egyptian. On the car ride to my aunt's house, where we usually celebrate Passover, I realized the irony of the situation.

The whole concept of Passover is to remember the days when the Jews were enslaved by the Egyptians. I grew nervous as we drew closer to the clapboard house in which my two aunts and their son live. I wondered whether Lora would feel comfortable celebrating a holiday of another religion.

Why Is Your Best Friend Your Best Friend?

I worried about how I would act in front of a friend and family, since I tend to act differently with each. I worried about how I would balance the identity I had established amongst my family members with the identity I had established amongst my friends.

But being at my family seder with a friend actually helped me to come out of my shell. Everyone welcomed my friend warmly. They held her hand through each stage of the seder, the ceremony that Jews perform on Passover. Everyone listened raptly as she shared bits and pieces of her culture and religion. "I don't eat pork either," she said excitedly.

I think the trick to being a well-rounded person is establishing a balance between the way you are when you're completely comfortable and the way you are when your comfort level is being tested.

Having my friend come to Passover dinner helped me to realize that I hadn't been balancing my two identities enough. My friend's grace among people she didn't know, practicing religious customs she wasn't familiar with, showed me that I need to carry the comfort I have with my friends into my family life. ■

Writing Prompts About Important Life Events

PROMPT
Describe Your First Love

Comfortable

Naomi Martinez

I can still remember the day I met him. Right from the start we knew that we belonged together.

He made me feel so comfortable when I was with him. He understood my problems when nobody could. He was always there in the nick of time when I needed him. And whenever I was depressed he would hold me in his arms until I fell asleep. He made me dream of a brighter day. He would tell me everything was going to be alright. He kept me safe and warm till the morning light. I would wake and there he'd be. He'd beg me to stay. But I had to go.

He stayed with me when I caught the flu. He took care of me when nobody else would. He stood by me when a boy would break my heart and I needed to cry. I hope by now that you know that this is not someone but something, and this something is my bed.

■

PROMPT

What's the Greatest Natural High You've Ever Experienced?

The Cool Caribbean Days

Ashlyn Celestine

I can remember the time when I felt free and alive without pain or sorrow. It was a time when the days just came and went.

It was a place where you could smell the sweet breeze of the ocean. Where the clouds were as white and fluffy as cotton. Where you could see hundreds of black birds flying in the air. At night the sky would be filled with stars—bright stars, dull stars, big and small stars, especially falling stars.

I would see caterpillars turning into beautiful, colorful butterflies. Families sitting on their steps drinking their morning cocoa. Dogs running up and down in each neighborhood yard.

Children would play a lot with their friends, eat with them, lie in the mud, get bathed under the hot sun in their underwear, and climb trees. They would even get into fist fights, though they knew they would get punished by their parents if they ever found out.

Saturdays used to be my hard working fun days. I had to do so much work it actually ended up being fun. I had to clean the house, wash the dishes, sweep the yard, scrub the concrete (it had to look almost white), feed the pigs, clean their pen, and when I was finished doing all of that, I went to help in the shop, where I got to meet almost all of my friends, when they came shopping.

I remember times when I ate so many plums and mangoes I wasn't able to eat my own food. Days when I would go to school with no shoes on my feet, red ribbons, a blue skirt and white shirt.

Each morning everyone would leave the house with a well-ironed white shirt, but would return with dirty ones. Your shirt would be so dirty your parents would think you just visited a pig-pen, with half the buttons gone and ashy feet.

Those days were wonderful. They weren't filled with crime, sex, and drugs, but rather with fun, love, and enjoyment that will never be lost, even if I travel a million miles away. Those were the cool Caribbean days. ∎

WHY IS YOUR BEST FRIEND YOUR BEST FRIEND?

PROMPT

What's the Scariest Thing that Ever Happened to You?

A Gun to My Head

Lynn Simon

In my life, I've had many frightening experiences, but the one I found most horrifying was what happened to me when I was attending night school at my old high school. Every night three special buses would wait in front of the school to take the students home.

Unfortunately, one night, my teacher let my class out a few minutes after the bell rang. By the time I got outside, the buses were gone. I had no other choice than to walk to the nearest bus stop. While waiting, I spoke to a fellow student who also missed the bus. As we spoke, we suddenly heard a lot of screaming and saw everyone running.

By the time I could turn around to see what all the commotion was about, trouble had struck me head on. I was about to meet my fate! An arm grabbed me around the neck and a gun was held to my head. I immediately became terrified and started to scream and cry. I also started to beg for my life.

The more I screamed and cried, the tighter the grip became. As this happened, I began to lose hope, thinking I would definitely lose the best gift I received from God—my life! I closed my eyes to pray and when I opened them, everyone—including my school mate—was hiding behind cars, looking on. In my mind I asked, "Oh God, why me?"

At this point, a man who appeared to be in his early 30s walked over, slowly, kindly pleading for the man who held me hostage to let me go. But the man lashed out, yelling, "If you come any closer, I'll kill her!"

Upon hearing those words, I became very angry and a sudden burst of courage came over me. I then said as calmly as I could, "Why don't you kill me and get it over with? Take me out of the misery of seeing my final minutes." As I said that my voice had deepened with rage. He didn't answer and for some strange reason, I didn't care anymore. Now that I think about it, I actually believe I meant it.

I felt as if weeks had gone by, without the sun coming up. But in reality, only a couple of minutes had passed. By this time, I had calmed down. I began to realize that losing my temper would not help me, only get me killed, and deep in my heart, I knew I really didn't want to die.

I also didn't know what was wrong with the man to make him act that way. He could have been mentally ill or a victim of hate and crime. He could also have been a cold-hearted murderer who didn't care about life or society. Due to the unknown, I didn't want to anger him more. So I decided to take what I felt, at the time, to be the smart approach. I asked him kindly to let me go. I tried to convince him that keeping me there was not going to help him.

As I pleaded with him, I heard sirens. Someone had called the police! Although I felt relieved, I also became fearful of what he might do. As the sound of the sirens came closer, he panicked. He threw me to the ground and looked me straight in the eyes. Then he began to run.

Before he could get far enough to escape, the cops arrived. They immediately got out of their cars and ran after him. When they returned, he was in handcuffs. I then told them what happened.

Ever since that night, I feel uncomfortable alone on the streets. No matter how much I try not to, I still remember the incident and the raging, painful look in the man's eyes as if it was yesterday. The only good thing is that I don't have nightmares about it anymore.

I always knew how bad the crime in New York was, but I never thought it would happen to me—until it did! ■

WHY IS YOUR BEST FRIEND YOUR BEST FRIEND?

> **PROMPT**
>
> **Love or Money?**
>
> —If you had to choose, which one would you rather have: money and security, or love and affection? Why?
>
> —What would your life be like after you've made that choice? What would you be missing out on?

From Money to Love

Christina Marie Lopez

If I had been asked this question a couple of years ago, I would've (no doubt) chosen money. I thought money was the answer to every problem. I would even go so far as to say that I worshiped greenbacks, papers, moolah, cash, dough, cream. I could go on and on about this green paper, on which we put so much superficial value. One reason is that addictions were a major problem in my life. I was addicted to what I thought were the fine things in life. I had to have name brand everything, from socks to underwear. I used to take cabs to school even though I had a bus pass, because I thought buses were only for people who couldn't afford cabs.

I was also addicted to weed and cigarettes, but I couldn't hear of just buying a "nick" of weed and a 50 cent "Philly" or a pack of stogies. No, I had to buy a $20 sack of weed and a carton of cigarettes, or none at all.

Of course, this caused major problems in my life. My mom's hard-earned money was being eaten up by a greedy, money-hungry little witch—me. Money totally changed my personality, and it was hard for me to maintain friendships because I valued money more than people.

Now I'm more mature, and see things totally differently. I've learned a lot since I was 14 and 15. Today, I would hands-down choose love and affection. These are things you can't buy with all the money in the world and you shouldn't have to.

Being an ex-cash addict, I know both the good and bad effects of money, but love only has good and positive effects. It feels good when you have someone to love you and love back. You can't tell a $10 bill about your first kiss. And when you have a problem or something bad happens to you, you can't tell a $50 spot you're feeling depressed: all you can do is spend it. And you'll still feel down afterwards.

But you can always go to someone you love and tell them anything and instantly feel better just because you have someone to talk to, who'll give you a hug and assure you that everything will be OK.

With love anything is possible. It took me a while to learn this, but now I have more respect towards people, and I get more respect in return. Love is enough to keep me happy nowadays! Mainly because love can only grow stronger and deeper, while money can get you in some deep problems if you're not careful.

I used to think a friend was a dollar in your pocket, but now I see that a friend is love in your heart, and someone who is always by your side whether you have a dollar in your pocket or not. Love makes all things possible, and I'd choose love over a dollar or even $50 any day. ∎

WHY IS YOUR BEST FRIEND YOUR BEST FRIEND?

PROMPT

Bad Hair Days

(Describe the worst experience you've had at the barber's or hair stylist's.)

I Looked Like a Bald Chia Pet

Christina Marie Lopez

It was my boyfriend's birthday and I wanted to look like the bomb for him. No doubt I had to represent, so I went to the neighborhood hair salon. They had a rep for hooking you up and doing phat styles. So I went in and decided on a relaxer, wash, and set.

I let my bun out and, as my hair fell down my back, everyone admired my long locks (but not for long). As the stylist washed my hair, I remember thinking how much my boyfriend was gonna love my hair.

I sat down in the swivel chair I loved so much, and closed my eyes and listened to Mary J. Blige and Method Man singing, "You're All I Need." Never did I think that all I'd be needing after I left was a wig.

As she massaged the relaxer cream into my hair, the stylist asked me had I'd ever had a perm. I said no, so she said she was only gonna leave it on for 15 minutes. Within the first five minutes my scalp felt like it was on fire, but I didn't say anything because I figured it was supposed to do that. By the time 15 minutes passed I thought I was gonna die, not to mention that I thought I heard sizzling noises coming from my dome.

When she rinsed my hair out, she said, "Oh my God!" as clumps of my hair came out in her hands. I screamed and looked in the mirror. I had patches of hair missing everywhere. She said I had a chemical reaction to the lye. I started crying and she said with a few treatments, everything would be fine. She did what was left of my hair in a wrap, and I left looking like a bald chia pet.

No doubt it wasn't my man's best birthday, because instead of looking like the bomb, I looked like a bomb hit me. I look back and cry because I still have the scabs to remind me of the horror. ■

> **PROMPT**
> Describe Something One Of Your Teachers Has Done That's Had a Big Effect on You

She Wouldn't Let Me Slide

Silin Yang

I used to be a shy person, so shy that I couldn't risk raising my hand and answering even one question. Gradually it became such a habit that I didn't bother to figure out an answer and simply satisfied myself with the answers that were given by other students.

When I got to junior high school, most of the teachers let me get away with my lack of class participation, because even though I didn't talk, I did all of my paperwork. Unfortunately, after two years of that "comfortable life," I got a new history teacher and my nightmare began.

After she took over the class, I still kept my old habit of being the quietest girl in the room, but she seemed to pick me out the first time she laid her eyes on me. She always asked me questions or for my opinions no matter how much I avoided making eye contact with her, broke down in the middle of a sentence, or blushed from embarrassment.

I was sure that I hated her 100%. She was the most insensitive and uncaring teacher I had ever met. But then, why did I begin to feel that I had to study for her class every night before I went to bed? Why did I pay special attention to the grade she gave me? Why was I so excited about going to her class? One semester passed by and I finally admitted to myself: yes, she was an uncommon teacher, and yes, she meant a lot to me.

A new semester came. When I found out that she would continue to be my history teacher, I was so happy that for the first time in my life I raised my hand in class. I can still remember the surprise in her eyes, but she immediately gave me permission to answer the question. After I nervously finished this "historic mission," she beamed. It was more like a friend's smile or a mother's. Oh, how beautiful she was—so sincere, so kind, so encouraging.

I didn't realize I loved her until then. But now I know that I liked her from the first time she gave me the opportunity to answer a question. I just said to myself I hated her because I hated myself for giving her a lousy answer. In return for her kindness, I had disappointed her.

I guess that day was the start of my new life. I finally got the courage to go out of my own little world and share my feelings with others. I am still shy, but I no longer let that be an excuse for not participating. It's difficult to challenge one's own weaknesses and I know I could never have done it without her—my dear teacher, a helpful friend, and the mother figure of my life. ■

Why Is Your Best Friend Your Best Friend?

> **PROMPT**
>
> **What's the One Thing You've Done in Your Life That You're Most Proud of and Why?**

Taking a Bullet for My Mom

Kevin Dorisca

Like any other Saturday, me and my mom were driving to the market in the brand new Lexus she had bought a month ago. My dad died in a car accident so she is the only real family I have since I'm the only child. We are really close.

We reached the market and got out of the car. She parked the car really far from the market so we had to walk for a while. A man came running toward us, pointing a gun at us, yelling and cursing. He wanted the keys to the car.

My mother refused and he pointed the gun at her and before he pulled the trigger I stepped in front of her. The next thing I knew I was in the hospital finding out that I got shot in the lower shoulder blade and fainted.

One person saw what happened and called the cops. The cops caught the man.

That was the best thing I ever did because the way I stood in front of her, my shoulder was blocking the gun which was pointing at my mother's heart. If I didn't step in front of her she would have been killed. My arm was hurting but my heart would have hurt even more to see my mom die. ■

Writing Prompts About Important Life Events

> **PROMPT**
>
> What's the Most Unusual Or Dramatic Thing You've Done (or Can Imagine Doing) to Convince Someone to Go Out with You?

Peddling Peanut M&Ms

Elizabeth R. Deegan

Evan Flough and I grew up three blocks away from each other. We were inseparable, always going to the park together and eating at each others' houses. When we got a little older, we were going to the movies. It wasn't until the summer between my freshman and sophomore years of high school, when the Floughs moved to Jackson Heights, that it dawned on me how special Evan really was. I guess it had something to do with the distance between us. For the first time I really had a chance to miss him.

Once school began it got a little better. Evan still attended our high school so I could see him in the hallways and some days I could even take the subway part of the way home with him. But it wasn't enough. I missed him so much. When I found out that he joined the Student Organization (S.O.) I immediately did the same. I didn't yet have the courage to tell Evan how I felt about him, but at least I was able to hang out with him again.

The S.O.'s first project that autumn was to sell M&M candy to raise money for new gymnasium lockers. As soon as our S.O. organizer, Mr. Gonzalez, said this, I made it my mission to do my best and win Evan's attention and maybe even his heart.

My best was better than I imagined and my dedication to Evan was more apparent than ever. I brought the candy to school every day. In the morning, I would get up early to pack my lunch so that I could devote my time in the lunchroom to peddling my sweets at each table.

When I would usually read (or doze off) on the subway to and from school, I devoted that time to selling candy. (You'd be amazed by how many people will buy M&Ms in the early morning.) I traded chores with my sister so that she would wash the dishes and I was in charge of picking up my little brother at school. That enabled me to sell to the little elementary school children in the neighborhood.

Lastly—and this had to be the most strenuous—I would sit through my brother's Little League games and cram all of my homework into one hour so I could sell to the kids and parents at the games for two weeks. It was tough, but it paid off.

The day after everyone had turned in their envelopes of money, we had a small party of soda and chips and fruit in the S.O. office. Mr. Gonzalez announced which students had raised the most and guess what? Evan and I tied for second place! We each got gift certificates courtesy of the pizzeria down the street from our school and ribbons of merit.

That night we used our gift certificates and had an early dinner together. Before we separated at Evan's train station, we congratulated each other again. Going for our usual "friendly hug," our lips met and we kissed for the first time. That night is known as our first date.

Thanks to all that candy selling, I not only helped out my school, but I found my true love too. Evan and I were boyfriend and girlfriend for two sweet years after that and are still the best of buddies. His family has moved to New Mexico, but we still write each other letters and call each other on Christmas and laugh about the fact that we will always think of each other when we bite into a peanut M&M. ■

Writing Prompts About Important Life Events

> **PROMPT**
> When Was the Last Time You Cried and Why?

Good-Bye, Imani

Stefani Gooding

When was the last time I cried? Truthfully, yesterday. Actually, I cry every day now.

It's been a little over a month since my little sister passed. Imani was her name and she was only 3 years old when she died.

Imani left us on September 25, two days after my birthday. Her birthday was less than a month away; she would have been 4.

I remember as a little kid always asking for a sister or a brother because I was lonely. When I finally got one, she didn't stay for even four years. Now, I am an only child again.

It's hard now because whenever I see a baby in a toy commercial or a magazine, I think about who I lost—my little sister.

Last night, my little cousin, who is 3, asked me on the phone if Imani was there. I said no. Then he asked me where she was, and I told him that she was in heaven. He asked me why, and I told him I didn't know why. I don't. I don't know why she isn't here with me anymore.

It's sad because there are so many things that I will never be able to do. I'll never be able to pick up my little sister from school, or see her graduate kindergarten, or show her how to do her homework. I'll never be able to experience those things.

One morning after my father and I had left the house for school and work, Imani just stopped breathing. My mother had finished bathing her and was drying her off.

Why Is Your Best Friend Your Best Friend?

When I left the house, I told her I loved her. Those were the last words I said to my sister.

The next thing I knew, they were picking me up from school and telling me that my sister was gone.

In my speech class, the teacher was talking about persuasive speech tactics and one of the tactics he described was fear. The opening of his speech on CPR was, "How would you like to see a loved one die because you didn't listen to this speech and couldn't perform CPR to save them?"

I don't think I will ever use that method of persuasion. If that were the case, then my sister would still be here.

My mother is a nurse and is required to have a license in CPR. Therefore, she knew how to perform it, and did, but my sister still died right in her arms that morning. Ironic, isn't it? And sad, too.

People keep telling me that it will get better, but I don't see how. I guess I'll just have to take it one day at a time. ∎

Writing Prompts About Important Life Events

PROMPT

How Was Your First Kiss, Or How Would You Want It to Be?

My First? The Worst!

Victoria Perez

My first kiss was the most humiliating moment of my life. It happened when I was in the 8th grade with a boy who was older than me.

When we started dating, I kept avoiding his attempts to give me a kiss on my mouth. Every time he would walk me home I would give him a kiss, but only on the cheek. I only kissed him on the cheek because I was scared of making out with him and I didn't know how to.

One day while we were in school he came out of his class and looked for me in the other rooms. When he found me he called me outside to the staircase, and we started to hold hands and talk for a while.

Soon it came time to say goodbye. I went to give him a kiss on the cheek, but he turned his head and started making out with me. He was moving his tongue in my mouth, and I just stood there because I didn't know what to do. I left my mouth and eyes open.

After the incident on the staircase, I felt humiliated because he told all of our friends that I didn't know how to make out. We broke up after my first kiss and I haven't spoken to him since. ∎

PROMPT
What Is Your Biggest Regret?

I Couldn't Express My Feelings

Amy Honigman

In sixth grade, I started a new school.
I walked through the halls, lost like a fool.
The halls were bigger, the people were too;
I hated being lost, hated being new.
A girl approached me and said, "Hi, I'm Jill."
She was brave to approach me, and it was really a thrill.
And on that first day, we talked and we talked,
and when class was over, together we walked.
The teacher put us together, it was an anonymous pick,
but I knew it was right, I felt it click.
From that day on, Jill and I were tight.
We talked and hung out, had an occasional fight.
People said we were cliquey, neither one of us cared.
We had other friends, but there was something special we shared.
She was like a sister, it was too good to be true,
then one day, it came out of the blue:
"I'm moving to New Jersey," like a knife through my heart.
How could she do this, just break us apart?
"When?" I asked. "When the school year is over?"
"Where are you moving?"

Writing Prompts About Important Life Events

"I am moving to Dover."
We didn't talk about it, didn't talk it through,
I thought if I forgot about it, it wouldn't come
true.
But that didn't work, and now she was leaving the
next day.
We were going to Six Flags with our class, then
she would go away.
While we were at the park, we fought, about what I
forget,
and this is why I have my biggest regret.
The fight was stupid, I forget the facts
but on both our lives, it made a lasting impact.
She wanted to go on the African safari,
we both knew we were wrong, but we couldn't say
"I'm sorry."
I am stubborn and I don't admit when I'm wrong.
Until then I didn't think it would affect me in
the long.
But I think there was more than that petty fight.
It was about what was going to happen
that night.
It was the easy way out, not to have to say
goodbye.
We didn't want to deal with leaving, see each
other cry.
But that was immature, I should express the way I
feel,
trying to hide it did not help me deal.
I tricked myself and said I didn't care
but when she left, it felt even more unfair. ∎

PROMPT

If You Were to Die Today, What Would Your Friends and Family Say About You at Your Funeral?

'She Felt Best When She Saw Other People Happy'

Channell Brooks

"Um, Mrs. Brooks, we have to bring the coffin out," says the funeral director.

"Okay, can you give me one more minute?"

"Yes."

The funeral director leaves and my mom continues to stare at me. She fixes my hair a little and says, "I always thought it was going to be the other way around. Many parents never let the thought of their children dying before them surface in their minds. I will never forget you no matter how old I get, and I will always love you."

She kisses my forehead and walks away. I love you too, Mom.

As I watch my coffin being pushed out to where all the guests are, I really start to think about how I'm going to miss everyone, but in the end—not to be all morbid—I'm sure I will be able to see them and speak to them again.

The funeral starts.

My dad speaks: "I'm not one who usually shows my emotions, but today I can't hold them in. She was my first child and her mom and I separated when she was 3. Even though she had problems with depression, I hoped that since we were both there for her she would be all right. But I feel I should have showed a little more love. She would always try to give me a hug and I would always push her away. I never really told her that I loved her, so I would like to take this opportunity to say something to her because I know she can hear me...I love you, Channell."

My friend Kathleen speaks: "I will be speaking on behalf of all of Channell's friends. She was the nicest, caring, most honest friend that we have ever had. Channell always kept us laughing even when a situation wasn't all that funny. She once told me that she felt best when she saw other people happy and enjoying themselves. That's where she got her joy from."

"She was a unique individual, through the way she thought, her music, style, movies, and eating habits (smirk). She once told me, 'A friend will give you the shirt off her back; a true friend will give you a clean one.' Thank you for listening."

My mother speaks: "I knew I couldn't get through a speech without crying (takes a deep breath, holding back tears), so I have prepared a musical selection for her. Channell loved the violin and I have asked a violinist to play 'The Dance of the Sugar Plum Fairies.' She really liked this piece, and I bet if we all close our eyes and listen, we will all capture a part of her for eternity."

The violinist begins to play and everyone closes their eyes... including me. ∎

PROMPT

What Is the Most Embarrassing Thing You've Ever Done and Why?

Caught Red Handed

Arneeka Paulson

The most embarrassing thing I've ever done was get caught stealing. It happened a couple of years ago with my friends. I admit that it was wrong and I knew that, but the thought of actually getting away with it really got to me so I went along. All the clothes in the store were pretty affordable but I didn't want to pay. Plus, my friends were amping me up. The store had cameras so employees knew exactly what we were up to.

Getting caught was embarrassing enough, but the manager actually walked all of us through the entire store just to get to the basement. They made it very obvious that we were trying to steal from their store. They threatened to call the cops and they even took our pictures. All the customers were looking at us like we were criminals. I was so scared I started crying.

At the time I didn't have a phone, so they wanted my address. I told them the truth and lucky for me they mixed up what I was saying and wrote down the wrong address so they couldn't send a complaint to my house. My mother ended up finding out about it anyway, not from the store, but from me. I was so scared I confessed to her myself. ■

Writing Prompts About Important Life Events

PROMPT

What Song or Movie Best Reflects Your Life, and Why?

No Happy Holidays

Tenisha Riley

The song that best reflects my life is "No Happy Holidays," by Mary J. Blige. The chorus in the song represents my relationship with my father.

I barely saw my dad when I was growing up. He even labeled himself a "Toys 'R Us Dad," because when he did see me he would make up for when he didn't with toys, clothes, and money.

As a kid I had no problem with that; I just thought that my daddy bought me anything I wanted. Now as a young lady, I know that his spending time with me was more important than any material goods.

In Mary's song "No Happy Holidays," she talks about how little she'd seen the love of her life, but in my case it's how little I've seen of my father.

She sings in the chorus: "Christmas you were with me/ New Year's Eve you were not around/ Valentine's came and went/ It makes me wonder where your time is spent/ Fireworks on the 4th of July/ Thanksgiving was another lie..."

I can relate to those lines so much. Now don't get me wrong, I love my father, but now that we can't spend time together it makes me think of the time I've missed.

On Christmas day, my father always came through with everything I asked for. He was a real life Santa. The following holidays

Why Is Your Best Friend Your Best Friend?

I would hear from him and he would promise to come but those days would come and go.

I began to wonder where all my father's time was spent. My father was always a busy man with a lot of people to take care of, but (not to sound selfish) I should have been his first priority.

Thanks to dear old dad, I have six younger siblings spread throughout the United States! So aside from his work, all the holidays had to be split among us. During my junior year of high school, I began to feel jealous of one of my little sisters who lives down south. It was like my father spent most of his time with her because it was more convenient.

There has been a birthday or two where he hasn't even called until two days after and there is a part in Mary's song that relates to that too. She says, "Valentine's Day I didn't get a heart to say 'I Love You,' I didn't even get a phone call."

I'm older now, and I'm also wiser. But just when I started to learn how to deal with my jealousy, they took my father away. The real world caught up with him. Now we can't spend time together. So all you dads out there, take a word of advice from me: Enjoy your children while you can. ■

Writing Prompts About Important Life Events

PROMPT

What Is the Most Spiteful Thing You've Done or Had Done to You? How Did It Make You Feel, and Why?

My Sister Made Me Her Slave

Tariq Assad

I was in the 6th grade when my sister blackmailed me out of spite. She got an "F" on her history paper, and I told on her. She wanted to get me back for getting her in trouble, and one day she did.

I went into a store to get some candy with some friends after school. My sister was in the store too, but I didn't see her. Then one of my friends said a curse to me. After that, I yelled the "F" word at him. My sister then jumped out from the aisle and said, "Aha! You said a curse!"

My mother didn't allow us to curse at such a young age. I told my sister not to tell our mother about it. She said I would have to be her slave for a week. I said no, but Jackie said she'd tell our mother. I had no choice but to be her slave.

I had to do her laundry, her math homework, make her food and get water for her from downstairs when I would be upstairs.

I was so exhausted from doing all those things, and it was only the second day of being her slave. Still, I continued being my sister's slave for another three or four days.

The fourth day was the worst. Jackie made me paint my nails black and go to school. But when I got there, I put on batting gloves so no one would see. It was still humiliating.

When I came home from school, she then made me paint her

finger nails pink. It was so boring. I would rather have gotten in trouble with my mother than do the things she made me do.

Then, worst of all, she told me to paint her toenails. That was the final straw. I wasn't going to be her slave anymore. I told her to go paint her own toenails. So she went and told our mother I cursed.

The funny part was I didn't get into a bit of trouble. My mother just told me that I shouldn't curse anymore. And Jackie got in trouble for making me her slave. ■

PROMPT

What's the Hardest Thing You've Ever Had to Do? Explain.

Learning English

Abu Nazakat

The hardest thing I've ever had to do was to learn English. When I came to America 11 years ago, I was 7 and in the 3rd grade. Even though I hated school because I didn't know how to speak English, I still had to go every day.

In the first two months my classmates came up to me and asked me questions, like "What's your name?" or "Where you from?" But I didn't know what they were asking me. I just stood there looking at them, like an idiot.

Meanwhile, I was always very quiet in class. But the kids tried to teach me curse words to say in front of the teacher or to other kids.

I was also scared to go to my gym class because sometimes the gym teacher asked all the students to get into groups. "We don't want you in our group," everyone hollered at me when I went up to them. Even though I didn't understand the language, I still knew by their facial expressions that I wasn't welcomed in their group. I didn't know what to do, and didn't understand the games.

At lunchtime, when all the other students were sitting with their friends and talking, I was alone. I didn't like to go to the lunchroom. I was scared. I thought other students might make fun of me. When it was time to go outside to play, I had no one to play with. When I saw the kids playing with their friends, it reminded me of my friends and school in Pakistan. I missed them a lot.

WHY IS YOUR BEST FRIEND YOUR BEST FRIEND?

In school there was another girl who spoke the same language as me (Urdu). I didn't like her because when the teacher asked her to translate for me, she talked very crudely.

"Don't you understand?" or "Are you dumb?" she'd say in a boorish voice. She was never nice to me.

Most of the time my teacher wrote a note for my parents about the homework assignments. My father, who spoke and understood English very well, would explain everything to me. He helped me with meanings and how to pronounce the words.

My teacher told my father that she could help me if I went to school earlier. The school started at 8:30, but I went to school at 7:45. My teacher helped me with writing and reading. She taught me the names of things and how to pronounce them. If I didn't understand something, she'd draw a picture or I'd understand by her facial expressions. It was very helpful.

In class, when the teacher wanted someone to read something, even though I knew how to read a little, I never raised my hand. I was afraid that other students might make fun of my accent.

"Trust yourself when you speak, and you won't be afraid," my teacher constantly told me.

About two months later, I started to make friends. Even though I didn't know how to speak English that well, my friends and I understood each other. I didn't know how to say whole sentences, so I just pointed at things or said some words in a broken sentence. But they always knew what I was trying to say.

I started to like my classmates, because they helped me with my class work and homework. In eight months, I started to speak English well. I learned English by working hard and getting others' help and persevering.

When I went to junior high school, I didn't have much of a problem speaking, reading, or writing English. I knew many kids in my school who came from other countries and didn't speak English, so I helped them. I knew how they felt in a new country. There were some kids who made fun of the way I spoke, but I ignored them and trusted myself when I spoke, as my teacher once had told me. "Would you be able to speak my language perfectly if you had to?" I asked them.

Now I'm 16 and I can speak English very well. I will never forget those two hardest months of my life. For me it was a whole new world. The people were new and the language was new. Now I understand that we can't learn something that fast. We have to try hard and should have confidence that we can do it. Nothing is that hard. Now when I look back to the questions my classmates used to ask, I wish I could answer them.

I think we should always respect other cultures and languages. We shouldn't make fun of other people. I like to help those who don't understand English and are new in this country. I feel happy when somebody needs my help and I'm able to help him or her. ■

Why Is Your Best Friend Your Best Friend?

PROMPT
Describe Your Best Or Worst Holiday Memory

'Santa' Took Gifts Out for Air

A. T.

I can remember a few times where a holiday or birthday didn't go exactly as I'd planned. On Thanksgiving I often ran around trying to make sure my parents didn't argue and that everyone was happy. On Christmas I usually tried to make my house look somewhat decorated so I could at least pretend that my family is festive.

The memory that stands out most is one Christmas when I was about 5, when my father took my presents "out for air."

Something about my family you have to understand is that my parents are constantly fighting. Usually the arguments are small and are forgotten in a matter of hours, but I really hate it when they happen on Christmas because that's supposed to be a family day.

That Christmas, we were staying with my grandmother. My parents had been bickering all day on Christmas Eve because my mother was not looking forward to spending Christmas Day cooking with her mother-in-law. They'd never gotten along and although we were living together, the situation hadn't gotten any better. Since my mother was complaining about my father's mother, it caused the argument to escalate.

My sister and I got exasperated and were determined to just sit in our rooms and ignore the "wacky adults." All we cared about was getting our presents the next morning and eating a great feast the next night. I wasn't concerned about what my parents were yammering about as long as Santa came and delivered my

Nintendo.

Now, my family has a way of changing well-known American traditions because we're all a little wacky, so instead of leaving cookies for Santa, my sister and I liked to leave popcorn. We went to bed that night all tucked in, wearing our red and green pajamas and thinking that Santa would be along any hour to deliver our goodies and eat the popcorn. However, those plans were dashed not even an hour after we'd fallen asleep.

I guess the argument had gone a little farther than my sister and I had thought because my father found it necessary to go and get smashed to try to forget about his troubles. My father only drinks when it's a holiday and when he is p.o.'d and I'm guessing he was really steamed to get that wasted.

He wasn't thinking clearly, so when he came back from wherever he'd been, raised voices in the hall woke up my sister and me. We ventured out into the hall and saw my father carrying several packages in his hands and looking extremely out of it.

"Carlos!" my mother snapped. "Where are you going with the kids' presents?"

"Uh... I was taking them out for air," he answered.

At this point, my sister and I were stunned and scandalized all at once. We figured out that a) there was no Santa Claus after all and my parents had been eating the popcorn all these years, and b) our father had been going to take our presents away because he was too drunk to remember that they were ours.

In short, this was my worst holiday memory because it was completely ridiculous and was a lousy way to find out that Santa Claus did not exist after all. There's probably something more serious I could've written but I decided that to me this was the worst and the most disappointing. Although it was unintentional, my parents took the magic out of Christmas for me as a kid. I'll always remember the night my father decided to take our presents "out for air." ■

WHY IS YOUR BEST FRIEND YOUR BEST FRIEND?

> **PROMPT**
>
> What Would a Movie Of Your Life Be About, And Who Would Play You?

This Boy's Life

Name Withheld

A movie about someone's life is seldom action packed with fight scenes or high-speed pursuits. (Well, it depends on who you are.) But my life isn't any different than any other person's. The majority of the fighting scenes take place in my thoughts and decisions.

If I had a chance to share my life with the world, I'd do it through a movie. If someone other than myself were to play me, I'd want it to be John Leguizamo, because a lot of people say I remind them of him.

The beginning of my movie would be a blur. Nothing would make sense quite yet, just as things never do to an infant. The couple who feeds you, stands over you while you try to sleep, and changes you, are strangers. But they grow on you and teach you little bits of useful information like, "Fire is hot," and "Don't put the fork in those little holes in the wall."

After many lessons learned and four years pass on, you laugh in your room thinking they're playing again. Things fall, and you run to their room to watch them wrestle like you and big brother do every week, but they do it more often. Mom always loses because she'll be crying when she comes to hug you, to tell you "I love you," and "Everything's going to be OK."

You never understand why until bags are packed with some of your clothes in them and you're ready to get far away from your father, to Puerto Rico, to live a new life. But years later, you'll figure out why things went the way they did.

So dad's gone, and you miss him so much, because you live in a place where the only people who understand you are the people you live with. There's a year of isolation because of your language impairment, which makes school a lot harder than it should've been.

At age 5, you come back to New York City, to the apartment you started in, to find that all your belongings are gone. And you and your mom (because your brothers live in Puerto Rico now) kind of realize that there's something wrong with the situation you're both in.

Then a year of homelessness passes with a horrible lesson for an innocent and inexperienced mind as yours, and you don't know what to think of anything anymore. Another year passes and things look up a little more than before. Mom meets someone. He takes you both in and takes care of you. Now you've got everything you need—food, clothes, school supplies, etc.

But then "It" comes into our lives, an unexpected house guest. Alcohol intoxicates their minds for too long to realize what they're doing, or what the alcohol's doing to them. Emotions are sent into an uproar, and there go the games mom used to play with dad, except now it's with someone else. In addition, now you're a part of the game, and now you're both crying.

You finally get a break after six long hard years, moving to your own apartment with your mom and everything seems nice, perfect! Until your mother meets another guy with the same problem. (It's funny how history repeats itself.) And it's back to the games that my father used to play, for another three years.

School's not easy for your uneasy mind that can't find closure within yourself. Therapists say it's not your fault—"It had nothing to do with you"—and all that's on your mind is that they're just saying that. Everything you love becomes everything you loathe. You find pleasure in pain, self-inflicted wounds, and looking for love in the places you never wanted to go. You followed the path you swore you'd never go.

I never said my movie was going to be a nice movie, but that's life. I'm not the only one who goes through hardships, and my life is no exception to the general population. If I were to make a movie about my life, though, I'd to try to make a change in the way people go about things. I'd show that other people's actions, as well as yours, make a difference. ■

Writing Prompts About Important Life Events

> **PROMPT**
>
> What's a Mistake That You've Made That You Don't Regret? Explain.

I Made Him Cry

Francisco Gonzalez

My mother walked into my room and said four words which would change my actions forever: "Lo isiste llorar, sabes." ("You made him cry, you know.")

Moments from that day appear in my memory, with certain parts crystal clear and other parts shrouded in mystery. Yet no matter how much of that day I accurately recall, I will never forget this one phrase.

I was rocking back and forth on the swing set behind my house, next to Alex Santos. Alex had always been bigger than me and had been my friend for as long as I could remember. From those earliest pre-school days, we were inseparable. I don't recall how or why we became best friends, but I do know that some of my earliest memories come from the days I spent playing with him.

I respected Alex for all of the qualities that he possessed which I lacked. He was braver than I ever thought I could be and more comfortable talking to people, especially girls. He was funny and usually managed to make everyone laugh. And though he made many friends over the years we hung out, he never left me. This is why it hurt me so much the day my mom told me what my words had done.

We were into one of our insult wars, which we waged whenever our parents were out of the room. We never took it seriously, at least until that day. We were both quick thinkers, and to us the war had simply been a form of recreation.

But on this day, Alex dug out the heavy artillery and insult book. As a result, I was forced to move past the old standbys into more original forms of cut downs. No "tu mama" cracks would hold up against him today. I was in for a fight.

But shortly after we began, I realized I was losing. I began to panic. I was reaching for something, anything which would act as a final, crushing blow. In a daze, I blurted out, "Oh si, pues tu tartamudeas." ("You stutter.")

That one phrase shut him up for good. It made me the clear winner. Sure it was mean, attacking the weak spot we both knew he had, but never spoke of. But we were only playing around, or so I thought.

Alex soon left to go home, in defeat. I didn't think that I'd ever hear of it again and had put it completely out of my mind until my mother came into my room later that night to tell me what I'd done.

After hearing her words, a shocking image suddenly hit me of this boy, my first true friend and the first person outside my family whom I respected, hunched over and weeping. This moment, which I had brushed off as nothing, affected Alex profoundly, and I hadn't realized it. I claimed to be Alex's friend but had been blind to the pain he experienced because of his speech impediment.

To me, the comment was a joke, but to him it had been a harsh insult, and had cut this brave, imposing boy more than I could've imagined.

Of course, I apologized to him immediately and told him that I hadn't known what the impact of my comment would be. All was soon forgiven. However, at least as far as I was concerned, all was not forgotten. Although Alex eventually stopped stuttering and later moved, I've often replayed that moment in my mind. For me, it serves as a reminder of the terrible power I can have over another person's feelings and of the need to think about my words before I speak.

But, most importantly, this moment showed me what it was to needlessly hurt another human being. It's as easy as making him or her feel terrific.

Even though I made a big mistake, it allowed me to learn a valuable lesson. Since that time, I've made an effort to be careful with my words and actions. Alex Santos probably doesn't remember the day I made him cry, but I've never been able to forget it, the imprudent attitude I had when I told him of his flaw, the shock I felt when I learned of the result, and the decision I made to see that it would never happen again. ∎

PROMPT

What's Something You Hide From People That You Secretly Want Them to Know? Explain.

I Love Women

Anonymous

"What's wrong?... What's wrong?... What's wrong?" The voices of those around me ring like church bells on a Sunday morning. "Nothing," is all I can ever tell them. I can't muster up the courage to tell them that I'm scared: scared of living, scared of surviving, but, most of all, scared of being me.

I was in love with my 2nd grade teacher, a very beautiful woman. I would do everything to please her. I was so in love with her that I learned how to spell "supercalifragilisticexpealidocious" just so she could give me a pat on the back. I just wanted a sign that she loved me as much as I loved her.

Students started calling me "teacher's pet" and "suck up," but that didn't bother me. What bothered me was when they started calling me "homo" and "dyke." I heard my father use the word "homo" before, so I knew what they meant. I was so confused though, because I couldn't see what was wrong with loving someone of the same sex. I thought that my love for my teacher was so pure.

My attraction to women continued to grow, but my willingness to tell people diminished. Then I fell in love with a good friend in 9th grade. We met in the school cafeteria because she thought I was lonely, which I was. I hadn't made any friends because I'm a weird girl. Still, she sat across from me and started talking to me as if we were two old friends.

We talked about everything, from books to teachers. I learned that she loved to read as much as I did. I knew that she was a girl with taste. I knew I was in love.

From that day forward, we hung out every day. We grew closer. I realized that because of our closeness, I had to be honest. I wanted to tell her that I was a lesbian and that I was in love with her. I waited many days and weeks. I wanted to tell her at the right moment, but it never came.

So one day, in my frustration to get the truth out, I shouted, "I'm gay!" It was the most liberating feeling that I've ever experienced. I told her of my love for her and, even though she didn't love me in the same way, she told me that she was still my friend.

I wish I could come out to my parents. I wish they could just hug me and understand that their daughter has not changed. I wish I could say that someone like Amber Benson (Tara from "Buffy the Vampire Slayer") or Julia Roberts is hot without having my mother scream at me. If I had the chance to come out and know that I am still loved unconditionally, I'd tell my family that I am a 17-year-old, Haitian-American queer woman. Then and only then would I no longer be scared of living, scared of surviving, scared of being me. ■

PROMPT

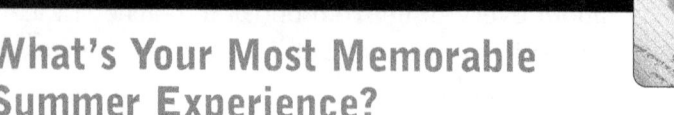

Worst Camp, Coolest Brother

Daniel Canter

My most memorable summer experience started off as my worst summer experience. It was the year I turned 10, and, like previous years, my mother and I scrambled for something to keep me busy during the summer. I was too young for a job, I didn't need summer school, nor could my mother afford sleep-away camp.

So my mother decided to send me and my 13-year-old brother to a new camp called Urban Pioneer Camp. The description said that campers would learn about and appreciate the environment. That's every child's worst fear, learning in the summer. But thanks to my brother, I would never have to do it.

The camp was awful, my brother and I soon realized: the counselors were either corny, lazy or both (except for one), and the activities the camp coordinator had scheduled were low-budget and tedious. One main activity was to build a shelter out of nature and a garbage bag so that when it rained we could go under it. We never finished despite several attempts. Every time we set up a foundation, someone tore it down.

One day when it was raining, my brother yelled out jokingly: "Head for shelter!" The shelter didn't have a roof and everyone got soaked, except for my brother, who had an umbrella that protected me from the rain as well. He told the camp coordinator, "It took you two weeks to build an unusable shelter when it took me two seconds to open this umbrella."

For the rest of the summer I hung out with my brother, sometimes sneaking into Sports Camp, which was next door. My brother didn't do the scheduled activities at Pioneer Camp and often disobeyed the counselors; the rest of the campers and I soon followed.

After about three weeks, two of the four counselors quit, as well as several campers. In fact, only about two people really liked the camp: the coordinator and one camper. The camp was never to be heard of again.

No, my most memorable summer experience wasn't the crappy camp. It was the time I spent with my brother and how it improved our relationship.

Before camp, my brother and I had no real relationship. I looked up to him, but he wanted nothing to do with me because I was younger than him. The camp forced us to be together and for that I'm thankful. To this day, the relationship I have with my brother is very close. I owe it all to the memorable summer of my 10th year. ■

WHY IS YOUR BEST FRIEND YOUR BEST FRIEND?

> **PROMPT**
>
> If You Could Go Back in Time And Change an Event in Your Life, What Would It Be? Why?

Tormenting Grandpa

Irving Caraballo

If I were able to go back in time, I would treat my grandfather a lot better. About two and a half years ago, my grandfather came from the Dominican Republic to the United States to visit my family. He stayed in my house for about a month and a half.

My grandfather was a grumpy old man, and he annoyed me. Even though there was no particular reason for me to feel this way, I just did. I kind of hated him for no reason. I would treat him with no respect at all. At this time in my life I was misbehaving and just being a straight-up adolescent. I really didn't care about anyone but myself. I had so much anger in me.

There were times when I would actually do evil stuff to my grandfather. Right now as I'm writing this, I feel so ashamed that I actually did these things, like make fun of him when he did things around the house, tickle his feet while he was asleep, or flush the toilet when he took showers so that the hot water would pour on him, and he would get angry and start to scream.

There's one thing I never understood about him—he never confronted me about these childish, silly games. He knew it was me, but he paid no mind to it. I was such a terrible grandson.

I had gotten along with my grandfather when I was younger. He and I lived together when I was a child, and he taught me how to ride a bike and read in Spanish. Deep inside my heart I really loved my grandfather, but I never expressed those emotions.

So the sad part now is that my grandfather is dying of cancer at a nursing home in the Dominican Republic. This past summer I had a job at a nursing home and met a couple of the seniors there. I was astounded by how wonderful they are. I wish I had had a relationship like that with my grandfather when I was 12.

I feel so much guilt. Every time somebody in my family brings him up, I get sad and emotional. I'm so terrified of him dying before I express my real emotions to him. Now that I am more mature, I feel his pain and grief. Writing this has made me cry.

My New Year's resolution is to go see him before he dies and explain why I was such a hateful child. I wish God could give me one more chance. I would treat him with all the respect in the world. I really love my grandfather with all my heart and wish the best to him.

I hope this is a lesson to all you other teenagers. Always have respect for everyone in your life or it will come back to haunt you. In my case, it did. ∎

WHY IS YOUR BEST FRIEND YOUR BEST FRIEND?

PROMPT

What is the Funniest Thing That's Ever Happened to You?

Fake Fans in the Spotlight

Carla Candelas

My funny story occurred about a year ago at Otakon (an anime convention), where a very popular band in Japan called T.M.R. was making their first appearance in the U.S. My cousin and I decided to go to the concert with a few of our friends.

We ended up really liking their music, so after the concert we went to an autograph session to get a chance to meet them. We felt a little intimidated because that concert was the first time we had heard their music, and everyone else in the room was a long-time fan. We decided to try to blend in and pretend that we too had been big fans for years.

When it was our turn to get autographs, my cousin began crying hysterically to fit the part of an obsessed fan and I was the first person to ask the main singer Takanori for a hug and kiss on the cheek.

Apparently their manager took a liking to our "performance." He didn't know that T.M.R. had such big fans in the U.S. My cousin and I were leaving the autograph booth feeling mighty proud of ourselves and of the performance we'd played oh-so-perfectly, when the manager came running up to us with a camera crew.

They wanted to interview us to show all of Japan what great T.M.R. fans live in the U.S. We were sweating bullets because we didn't know what to do. In the end, we decided to go with the flow and allow them to interview us.

We played our parts perfectly until they asked us what our favorite song was. We had no idea what the titles of any of their songs were. My cousin and I stood there like a couple of deer in headlights. I can only imagine how our faces looked on the video.

We finally gave an answer after what felt like forever. The manager obviously could tell that we'd been bluffing the whole time and weren't as big fans as we had pretended to be. He stopped the video and shot us a look of disappointment. He and the camera crew left us in the middle of the convention feeling absolutely humiliated.

We thought they wouldn't show the video in Japan, but we were wrong. A friend sent us a link to the band's official website and right before my eyes was the video we were in.

Of course, they had cut out the scene where my cousin and I made fools of ourselves. Ironically, I can actually call myself one of their biggest fans now. ■

PROMPT

Write a Letter to Your Parents, Telling Them What's Going On in Your Life That They Should Know About—But Don't

My Boyfriend Hits Me

Dear Grandma,

I need to talk to someone because I need to get something off my chest. I know you told me if anybody put their hands on me I would have to handle my business. In this case I can't, because my boyfriend is too big and too fast for me to hit him back. And yes, I'm scared of him.

You always told me if I could avoid fighting, I should do so. So rather than try to hit him back, I asked him to tell me the purpose of hitting me. He said I got him upset because of something I did to him, that hitting me was his way of expressing his feelings of hurt and anger.

I told him that I understood that he was mad at me but that hitting me does not make matters better. I told him that putting his hand on me is pushing me away from him, and makes me not want to see or be with him anymore.

We're trying to communicate and work things out, but I guess I just wanted you to know what was going on in case things get really out of hand. I don't mean to worry you or to upset you, and I hope you understand how hard it is for me to tell you all of this. I just need to get through this, and be all right.

Cindy ■

Writing Prompts About Social Issues

> **PROMPT**
>
> What Does the American Flag Mean to You?

Hope

Ninh Mac

The waves used our wooden ship back and forth.

When we left the tumultuous part of Haiphong, Vietnam we had no idea where we were going. But we all understood the inevitable need to venture into the ocean. Unfortunately, the winds trapped our overcrowded vessel in dormant waters. After 11 days of aimless wandering, the passengers were growing fatigued and ill.

People were seasick and desperately needed food and fresh water. Children were crying, whether in fear or in hunger I could not tell, for I myself was still a child. Their somber, sallow faces held so much hope in their eyes, but they had so little hope of surviving.

The next night, a storm overcame us. Our ship was flooded with water and lightning had struck the mast. Wind and rain tore the vessel to pieces. Confusion and fear swept the crew. People who fell into the water struggled to find the light coming from the ship. Those who could swim remained afloat. And the children, whose cries were drowned by the waters, sunk into the deep, dark vacuum.

From out of the mist emerged an enormous warship. It dispatched lifeboats to rescue us. As an officer lifted me out of the frigid sea and onto his craft, I spotted the American flag, wet, yet waving proudly.

If You Could Bring Back a Dead Celebrity, Who Would It Be?

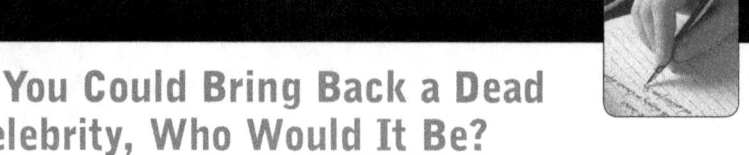

Martin Luther King, Jr.

Kiesha Osborne

I have a dream!

If I could bring any celebrity back from the dead, it would be a man who fought for what he believed in and believed in what he fought for. I am referring to Dr. Martin Luther King, Jr., a man who I believe was and is the greatest role model ever to have lived.

I would like to meet Dr. King on his birthday at one of the places named after him. I would like him to know that the people have not forgotten him or what he fought for.

After meeting Dr. King, I know that my greediness for his knowledge would be uncontrollable.

I have often wondered what Dr. King would think of our society as it is today. Would he be pleased, disgusted, pacified, or downright outraged?

I also wonder how Dr. King would feel about racism, as it is in our present society. Would he be silenced and accepting (after all, racism has decreased since his time) or would he be determined to totally eradicate this plague?

I believe that if Dr. King had lived he would have continued in his fight and perhaps racism would have been eradicated. Unfortunately we can never know for sure.

I greatly admire Dr. King, his work and his dedication. I don't know if anyone could ever follow in this great man's footsteps, but if I could bring anyone back from the dead it would definitely be him: THE MAN WITH A DREAM. ■

Writing Prompts About Social Issues

PROMPT

If You Could Solve One Problem Facing Teenagers, What Would It Be and How Would You Solve It?

More Jobs, More Games

Shamekia Gill

One problem I know teenagers are facing today is a lack of programs. A lot of the programs that we had are no longer around—because of budget cuts, that's what they say. But it's killing the kids in the communities. If there's nothing else for them to do, they're going to find something to do and most likely it's going to be in the streets.

What I would suggest as a solution is work programs—jobs where only teenagers will be able to work. And game rooms that they could come to every day after school with their parents' permission, where they would only have to pay half price for three games at a time. There should also be programs that parents can afford, where they can send their children for tutoring.

Together, all of these programs will solve a lot of problems on the streets. Less money would be spent keeping kids in jail and that money could go to keeping them off the streets. ■

PROMPT

What Should Teens Know Or Do Before Having Sex?

I Was Flooded with Unfamiliar Emotions

Shawnta Smith

Every day—whether it be from an ad on the bus, a counselor with diagrams and scientific explanations, or a pamphlet—teens are constantly being told about safe sex. Yet no one dares to speak of the emotional aspects of sex: the side that can't be taught, only experienced for yourself.

I thought I knew it all when I was about to have sex for the first time. I had contraception, and my calendar was scheduled to my personal cycle.

I even went to the length of visiting the doctor with my boyfriend, for thorough exams and tests for every sexually transmitted disease (STD) known, including AIDS. I know I may sound a bit obsessive, but after the counselor's pamphlets and teen pregnancy statistics, I couldn't take any chances.

Finally, my boyfriend and I were ready. Or at least we thought we were. But after having sex I felt devastated and so did he. Neither of us knew why. Was it guilt? Did we forget to do something? No! I will tell you what it was: just a different, very different kind of feeling. It wasn't bad, nor was it good, just different. Sometimes teenagers aren't ready for the emotions that take place during and after sex.

Fortunately, my boyfriend and I love each other. We weren't

ashamed to share and talk about the way we felt our first time making love. But for other people, I know it might not be that easy, whether or not it is their first time. They may have had sex with the wrong person for the wrong reasons, and may not be able to discuss or even understand why they feel the way they do.

From my experience, aside from contraception, teens should know that they are going to experience unfamiliar emotions that may have a lasting effect on them and, without a loving partner, having sex may not be as wonderful as making love. ■

WHY IS YOUR BEST FRIEND YOUR BEST FRIEND?

PROMPT

Should Marijuana Be Legalized?

Legalization Is a Drastic Resort

Lina Georgieva

I have not once been tempted into using marijuana or any other illegal substance and am a 100% supporter of all efforts aimed to help and educate teenagers in the battle against drugs. But unfortunately, with each passing day, it appears to be a battle that can't be won.

Use of marijuana has become a fact. Anti-drug abuse organizations set up for the benefit of troubled teens have been unsuccessful in destroying their curiosity and interest in marijuana.

Past events support my statement. Prohibition, from 1919 to 1933, proved unsuccessful, as gangsters like Al Capone emerged and bootleggers found ways to smuggle alcohol, despite the government's earnest attempts to stop them. As a result, the use of alcohol was legalized, since the attempt to make a "dry America" had sorely failed.

Despite the hazardous impact of marijuana, alcohol, cigarettes, and other such substances, laws that forbid their use are powerless to stop addicts. It is proven time after time that laws are constantly broken and that no law can be fully enforced on the public. Drug users will always find new ways of selling and using marijuana, despite the laws that forbid them to do so.

If marijuana is legally sold in pharmacies or hospitals, abuse of the substance could be spotted at an early stage. Common misconceptions and questions can be cleared up by professionals selling marijuana. They can ensure that the substance is authentic and will not cause damage to the user.

Legalizing marijuana is a drastic resort, but it may be worthwhile in the end if we manage to control the problem, rather than spend energy (in vain) in trying to completely abate it.

Those who smoke marijuana would much rather buy it from a pharmacy than in a dark alley. And think of all the drug dealers who will be put out of commission when that happens!

I'm not naïve enough to think that legalization will completely reduce crime and save lives, but I am positive that it will be a better solution to an unsolved, spreading problem. ∎

Imaginative Writing Prompts

PROMPT

If You Had Supernatural Powers, What Would You Do?

Make the World a Better Place

Jabbar Collins

I would fly over the oceans of the world using my x-ray vision to look for sunken treasure. I would bring these "gold mines' back to the U.S. to invest and stimulate the economy.

Using my super-hot eye beams I'd melt down metal into two gigantic cups and head straight for the nearest and largest garbage dump. I'd lower the giant baskets, getting two giant scoops of garbage. Then I'd zoom directly for the sun, releasing garbage so that it is zapped by the sun's massive heat. I'd continue to do this until the garbage dump was empty.

One by, one I'd clear out all the landfills in the world. Then I'd fly to Mount Rushmore and pound and carve, sand and smooth until the faces of Martin Luther King Jr., Nelson Mandela, and my mom and dad's faces are carved out right near the great presidents.

Even though people have no super powers, each person has her own power, the power to make this world a paradise by sharing, caring, and loving one another. ■

PROMPT

What Happens After We Die?

Is there a heaven? A hell? Something else? What does it look like? Feel like?

When You Die...You Die.

Jason Lloyd

When you die, you are put in a coffin and buried beneath the ground or in a mausoleum. Either way, your body is dead. You don't move, get reincarnated or resurrected, you just lay there, dead.

You don't feel or know that you're dead. Your soul doesn't float out of you and happily go to heaven and it doesn't miserably go to the fiery caverns of hell, either. You don't get little wings and fly around in the clouds or meet the devil while feeling the heat, fire, and evil around you. Your body just stays in the ground, undisturbed, and decays until only your skeletal remains are left.

You don't see a brightly lighted path leading you to the heavens, or a fire-filled black pit open beside you. The Grim Reaper doesn't fly over you with his spectacularly sharp scythe and drag you away to the dungeons of the dead.

When you die...you die. ■

Imaginative Writing Prompts

PROMPT

How Is the World Going to End?

With a Boom!

Christopher J. Figueroa

Andrew Stevens walked down the dirty marble staircase of his office building and out into the misty evening. His mood was vivid and flirtatious as he looked forward to the rest of the evening with his girlfriend, Laurie.

Driving in his car, Andrew turned on the radio and began listening to some music, when suddenly it was cut off.

"This is the emergency broadcast system. As of 4 p.m. this afternoon, the President of the United States has declared a national state of emergency. All citizens must immediately, I repeat, IMMEDIATELY, report to underground shelters, subways, or fallout shelters and await further instructions. This is the emergency broadcast system..."

Andrew couldn't believe what he was hearing. Already sirens could be heard in the distance and people were scrambling out of their cars to find shelter. Andrew immediately stopped his car, got out and began running with the crowd.

Stumbling and out of breath, he managed to make it to a subway station. It was stuffy and crowded and people were screaming for room and for answers. From the crackling of the loudspeaker it was clear that someone was about to speak. The entire station quieted down in order to hear the voice that was barely audible.

"May I have your attention please? We are currently in a state of national emergency. Russia, Germany, Czechoslovakia, Romania, and Iraq have threatened the United States with nuclear destruction. The President is at this moment negotiating with all parties in order to prevent this from occurring. We strictly advise all persons to find immediate shelter underground. Do not come out until notice is given to do so. We appreciate your cooperation. Thank you."

The static droned on like a tide of rushing water as the crowd stared at one another in bewilderment. Andrew couldn't believe what he had just heard. He found a small corner at the end of the platform and sat down, thinking only of his life and of Laurie, his only love.

Hours went by and Andrew fell asleep. He was awakened by sirens wailing in the night in the street above. The people in the station began panicking and pushing up against one another.

Somewhere in the distance, two extremely loud explosions sounded. The ground began to tremble, shake and crack as the first two nuclear bombs exploded over the city.

In the subway station, people were screaming hysterically. Some were even running into the tunnels to escape. Then horror struck as flames rushed down the stairs into the station and began torching everything that was combustible.

Andrew stared in amazement as the flames rushed in his direction. He knew all too well that there was nothing for him to do. He watched as the flames engulfed him and the pain took away every thought and every action. Then darkness overtook him and Andrew was no more.

Above, in the streets, buildings were shattered and torn. Bricks, cars, bodies, and everything else lay strewn in all directions. Flames burned green, orange, and sickly red. The temperature dropped considerably and the sky turned a deep red and lit up from time to time. The clouds churned in all directions. No one seemed to be left alive.

The entire country lay in ruins. Every major and minor city, every small town had been utterly destroyed. The Great Plains burned uncontrollably, along with the forests of the Rockies and the Appalachians. Where the bombs had detonated lay mile wide craters. Nothing moved. The United States had met its fate.

Due to the tremendous impact of more than 2,000 nuclear bombs, the shockwaves caused major earthquakes in all parts of the world. Tidal waves smacked the shores and surged miles inland. The entire globe began to quake. Cracks split much of the world apart until molten lava began shooting into space.

The cracks multiplied until an immense explosion caused the whole planet to blow up. The tremendous shockwave caused by the explosion obliterated the moon and knocked Venus and Mars out of their orbits. Mother Earth was no more. And for what? ■

WHY IS YOUR BEST FRIEND YOUR BEST FRIEND?

PROMPT

What Was the Weirdest Dream You Ever Had?

I Had a Cow

Edgar Muniz

Last week when I fell asleep on the train home I had the weirdest dream. I was going to the store for some milk. It was warm out; it was, let's say, 9:30 at night.

There weren't many people out—just beggars. The store I usually go to was closed, so I had to go to the next block. As I was crossing the street someone yelled. As I looked back, a car came screaming out of nowhere and hit me.

As I slowly got up, I was freezing. It was about 50 degrees out. A cow came over to me and said, "So, you want some milk, punk?" I was scared to death; he had a bat in his hand. He also had about 40 friends with him.

I told him I didn't want the milk, my friend did. When the cow looked away, I punched him in his face, making hamburgers out of him. The other cows chased me with chains and bats yelling, "Kill him."

One cow caught up to me and wacked me over my head with a chain. This hurt! I begged him to stop and to be merciful. Then I was surrounded. They all started beating me when a baby cow yelled. They stopped, so I ran quickly into a corn field.

I kept on running until I saw a car in the middle of the corn field. I hot wired it, threw it into drive. Then "BOOM," it blew up. I luckily survived, but what now? I couldn't believe this misery. And I thought Woody Allen had it rough. My head was still in pain.

Just then a spaceship landed. Three Martians came out smiling with M&M's in one hand and a laser gun in the other. I started to cry. All I wanted was to go home. One of the Martians said, "You are in the Milky Way Galaxy now. This ain't The Land of Oz." I yelled, "Help!" as they got closer and closer. Suddenly someone yelled. Next thing I knew the conductor of the train was yelling, "LAST STOP—EVERYONE OFF—THIS MEANS YOU." ■

> **PROMPT**
> Say It in Slang:
> If I Ruled the World...:

Mi Put De Chiran First

Marcia Benons Stoute

Ef mi was de 'oman who ruled de world, mi tink 'ould stress more tings un ed-u-ca-taion. First of all, de chiran 'ould all wear uniforms. Fom de first standud tu de 12 stanud. De chiran ed-u-ca-tion 'ould be de success to mi country. De teachin' of chiran 'ould begin learning' fom de age of one. Dis a show de chiran values an give dem a positive feelin' towads de futua. Dey will use dis knowledge, dat 'av bin planted, since dey small tu ovacum world problems: pollution, poverty, an 'omlessness. Dis is 'ow mi a rule mi world. "De chiran is de future." ■

Imaginative Writing Prompts

PROMPT

What Brings Out The Beast in You?

Greed

Myles Ramzee

There are a lot of beasts in me. One of my beasts is my hunger beast. My hunger beast comes out when I am hungry and my stomach growls. When I am hungry I don't want to listen to anyone. I just want to eat. I don't care if another person does not eat as long as I eat. And if I don't eat when I want to I will have an attitude and act like a baby.

But my most dangerous beast is the beast that caused me to sell drugs and help poison people with crack. This beast's name is "Greed." Greed visited me when I was 16 years old. I had many problems at home so I was very weak-minded and Greed knew that I was weak. He introduced himself to me. He looked very good. He was green and white and little. I didn't think he could harm me.

He said that he was God and "In God We Trust" was written on his chest, so I believed him. He said, "You can do anything with me." He told me he multiplies and I asked him, "How?" And that is when he introduced me to a substance called crack. He said, "Sell crack and you will see more of me and I will make you happy." I did what he said and it ruined my life.

This beast looked familiar after a while. I saw him with my mother and I asked my mother, "What are you doing with him? He ruined my life, he had me thrown in jail, he made me drop out of school, he made me hurt people, he almost made me run away from you, mother." And my mother said, "He is powerful, but Myles, you let him control you. There are other ways to meet him. He is not bad, greed is the bad one and if you don't let greed control you, you will be all right."

So I asked my mother, "Who is the little guy in green and white?" My mother said, "His name is money." Then money began to speak and he said, "Stay away from greed because greed caused you nothing but pain. I will always be here, so begin a new life and I will visit you again." ■

Imaginative Writing Prompts

> **PROMPT**
>
> If You Could Be Anybody
> In the World, Who Would You
> Be and Why?

Cupid

Colleen Chan

If I could be anyone in the world, I would choose to be Cupid.

I wouldn't choose to be the President or some great inventor. Eloquent speeches and technological gadgets may enhance life but they don't have the power to instill love in the hearts of others... and love is the only thing that can make this world a kinder place.

If I could be Cupid, I'd spread love all over the world simply by aiming a few arrows. I'd have the ability to change the world and truly make it a better place because love engenders respect, acceptance, and forgiveness.

War, crime, hate, greed, and cruelty are all fueled by emptiness. Love could fill this void and put the brakes on the oh-so-many problems that we face day after day. No law or speech or invention could ever generate the love and kindness that Cupid has the power to create.

When I started school, I discovered hate, indignation, and a pain in my heart that wouldn't subside. Whatever self-esteem and pride I had was taken away from me. The worst part is that my peers in grades 1 through 5 were the perpetrators.

This group of kids was led by a girl who I will never forget. She had tremendous hatred for me. I still don't understand why she picked me to prey upon. She teased and ridiculed me and went out of her way to make me feel as if my life wasn't worth living. I suffered but I gradually learned how to deal with the heavy lump in my throat that I had to carry with me each day.

I'm still curious as to why those kids, and especially that girl, could be so cruel. Maybe there really isn't an explanation but I do believe there is a resolution.

To me, being Cupid would mean being able to save others from that kind of suffering, regardless of their race, age, or gender. It would mean really bringing happiness to others and proving that love really does conquer all, not only on Valentine's Day, or around the holiday season, but always, every day. ■

Imaginative Writing Prompts

PROMPT

If You Had $10,000 And Only a Day to Spend It, What Would You Spend It On?

Make Grandma Queen for a Day

Nicole Wallace

I'm 19 years old and I live with my grandmother because when my sister, my two brothers and I were younger my mom took drugs.

Two years ago my sister was shot and killed by her boyfriend who is now in jail. My grandmother took on the responsibility of taking care of my sister's three small children—ages, 9, 5, and 4. She gets up early every day to get them ready for school. She cooks, cleans, and washes clothes. All of this and never does she complain. She's 66 and I think she is remarkable.

She helps everybody in my family in their time of need. She's the best thing that could have happened to us. She is the glue that holds my family together. Most of the time she goes unnoticed. So for once I would like to show her my love and gratitude for all that she has done for me. She gives so unselfishly that $10,000 could not begin to repay her, but it's a start.

At this time in her life, she should be relaxing and enjoying her retirement. Instead she works her fingers to the bone. So with my $10,000, I would make my grandmother QUEEN for the day.

First, I would hire someone to take care of the children. Then I would rent her a fancy car to drive her any place in the city that she wanted to go. If she wanted, I would charter a small jet to take her to another city for a shopping spree. I'd let her have lunch in the fanciest restaurant in town. I would have her pampered from head to toe in a beauty spa. And when she was done, I would have a hotel suite waiting for her where she could have dinner while looking out at a spectacular view of the city. And although her day would end there I know it would be a day that she would never forget. In my book she will always be a QUEEN. ■

Imaginative Writing Prompts

PROMPT

How Would It Feel
To Be Your Favorite Color?

Like a Lipstick Kiss

Genese Yearwood

If I could be red, I'd show the emotion of love. I'd be the roses that say, "I love you" and Valentine's Day. I'd be the heart that beats and the blood that races at the feeling of being loved. I'd be the red lipstick of kisses planted upon someone's cheek. I'd keep love in the palm of my hand. I'd be Cupid's right hand man. I'd include myself in the fun as everyone painted the town red.

If I could be red, I'd be history. I'd be the blood that was shed to shape the world into what it is today. I'd be the blood of soldiers and protesters who fought for what was right.

If I could be red, I'd be youth. I'd be the color of imagination and creativity. I'd be the Crayola crayon in a young child's hand that encourages the love of art. I'd be the red ink that flows from the pen that places the 100's and A+'s upon tests and papers, that motivates us to continue the endless process of learning. ■

WHY IS YOUR BEST FRIEND YOUR BEST FRIEND?

PROMPT

Describe the Night Time Through the Eyes of a 5-Year-Old

Good Night? Yeah, Right!

Joseph DiBiasi

I went to my window,
And looked out below,
Smoke and flames rose in the sky.
On the corner were people getting high.
You could hear shots close to the bay,
and sirens rang out, from far away.

And now finally the sun went down,
But that didn't quiet anything in this town.
I went to bed to sleep,
My thoughts drifted deep.

Bam! Oh no, what was that noise?
Maybe it was someone breaking my favorite toys.
Maybe it was Santa coming a week late.
Maybe it was a monster filled with hate.
What if it was under my bed?
Would it eat all of me, or just my head?

Squeak! What was that sound?
Was it a thief looking around?
Maybe it was the shoe of a clown.
Is he happy, or does he wear a frown?

'Cause everyone knows that it's the sad ones
Who cook you up and throw you on buns!

Crack! Now what was that?
Was it someone's tire going flat?
Or was it a big green alien?
Strange Martian men
Coming with their big ray gun?
Will they force us to work on the sun?

Dumf! What was it now?
It's coming closer to the bed's bow!
It's too dark to see!
Is someone trying to get me?

AHHH! It just started to attack.
What to do now, should I just sit back?
I really wish I had my bat
To use against this giant green alien... Cat?

Phew, it's just a harmless feline.
I calmed down and now I'm fine.
I put down my pet,
Turned off the TV, and I was set.

Good night to all, good night to dad,
Good night to mom, I'm tired and I'm glad,
Good night to my cat Fred,
Most of all good night to the monster
under my bed! ■

> **PROMPT**
>
> If You Could Have Someone Be Your Personal Slave for a Day, Who Would It Be?

The Governor

Marcel Beckford

If I could have someone be my personal slave for a day that person would be our governor.

This is because I view his proposed budget cuts to education as a method of keeping not only me but all our state's youth under mental slavery. I see our governor the same way the abolitionist Frederick Douglass saw his masters almost 200 years ago. Douglass once stated that he had been cheated out of knowledge and his masters tried to keep him in ignorance. That's what our governor's budget cuts will do to me.

I would make the governor actually live my life for a day. I would make him do everything I have to do from morning until evening. He would have to hop on a bus to school and while at school he would have to worry about the programs that are getting cut. Maybe then he would get a wake-up call. ■

Imaginative Writing Prompts

> **PROMPT**
>
> ## A Double Life?
>
> Clark Kent and Superman. Bruce Wayne and Batman. Dr. Jekyll and Mr. Hyde. You and...?
> Imagine there is a side to you that your family and friends don't know about, a second personality that could do things you don't usually do, go places you don't usually go. Describe this "other" you. (It doesn't have to be a superhero!).

Average, Normal, And Boring No More

Saraya I. James

You may not realize it but you probably know me. I'm sure you've seen me many times before. And chances are you didn't even notice me.

I live on your block, in your neighborhood. I shop at your supermarket and I go to your school. In the summer you probably play handball in the same park that I do and in the winter you probably ice skate at the same rink. Perhaps we've sat next to each other on the bus or the train. You may have even asked me for the time. But (I know, I know) you don't remember me, right? And why should you?

Well, let me introduce myself. My name is Average Normal Boring. My family and friends call me Prude. You still don't recognize me? Let me put on the scarf that always covers my hair. What if I put on my glasses and take off the makeup? Maybe if I don my husband's too-large clothes, as usual, and take off this chic outfit that accentuates my feminine "assets." It might even help if I went back into the house and only came out to pick up eggs and bread from the market, or haul the dirty clothes to the laundromat.

Oh, now you know who I am. Bet you can't believe your eyes. You thought you had me all figured out, didn't you? Yeah, I'm the married teenager who lives across the street in the run-down house. Yeah, I have a son who is now a year and a half. Yeah, I have no job, I was unable to attend college as planned, and I have absolutely no life. Not now. Not yet.

I've allowed life to trap me. I let my husband control me. I let him hit me, cheat on me, disrespect, and disregard me. I've let him use my love for him to destroy me and suck the hope out of me. I no longer laugh, I cry. I don't go out and pursue, I sit in and wish. I don't demand, I beg. I don't stand tall, I cower. I don't live, I simply exist. Sometimes.

Other times, like today, I cease to be Average Normal Boring a.k.a. Prude. Instead, I become Unusual Extraordinary Phenomenal. You probably didn't even know I had a side like that. A side of me that is strong and hopeful. A side of me that is in control. A side of me that actually lives! Yeah, well, I'm ready to come "out of the closet." Before today U.E.P. was living undercover, afraid. She was evident in words only: heated conversation, powerful prose. She was a denizen of dreams and fantasies. Today she is packing her bags and moving on to reality.

She doesn't wear a cape and tights and she can't fly. But she can regain control of her destiny and even help reshape the destiny of others just like her. She doesn't have to fall into the typical stereotype of a black, teenage mother. She can get a job, get an education, get a divorce, get a life! She can really be a Phenomenal Black Woman. ■

> **PROMPT**
>
> **Your Own Words?**
>
> If you could add a new word to the dictionary, what would it be and what would it mean?

Shizazz

Zaharah McKinney

Shizazz, noun. Definition: ultimate standard of beauty and excellence, used to describe anything admired or an action in which excellence is defined.

Example #1: The cutest guy you've ever seen walks by. In awe you say, "He is just shizazz."

Example #2: You sit under the stars with your boyfriend on a spring night. As he kisses you passionately, the feeling you get is simply "shizazz." ■

PROMPT

If You Could Adopt a Wild Animal, What Would It Be and Why?

A Monkey

Hoorya Riaz

If I could adopt a wild animal, I'd adopt a monkey. Monkeys are so cute and playful. They're full of tons of energy.

I'd put my monkey in a mini-house, similar to a dog house, and keep the house in my room. I'd take him with me everywhere I'd go. I would call him Abu because Aladdin's monkey's name is Abu. I'd have to keep a stock of bananas to keep the monkey alive.

If I could bring it to school, the monkey would attract a lot of attention. All my friends would play with it. I'd enroll him in high school and he'd have the same schedule as mine. Since monkeys learn fast, he'd get straight E's (for "excellent") in all his subjects. He'd be the teacher's pet.

My monkey would fight for animal rights and become a Muslim. He'd wear those white hats on his head and pray five times a day. He would run in my school's government elections and become student president. He'd be so smart that I'd have him do my homework. For the senior prom, he'd bring a gorilla for his date and would be the main attraction on the dance floor.

My life would definitely change if I had such a monkey. Many scientists would write to me, wanting to do research on why the monkey is so smart. ■

PROMPT
What Would You Do If You Only Had a Month to Live?

Indulge Myself

Amy Ho

If I only had one month to live, I would enjoy life to its fullest, as everyone would like to do. However, most people are not able to do so because they must work in order to make a living. Unlike them, I would no longer have to do anything I didn't want to do.

The first change in me would be my appetite. Instead of constantly struggling to control it for the sake of my physical appearance, I would finally let it control me and indulge: Ben and Jerry's ice cream and chocolate bars galore! Piecemeal portions would no longer suffice—I would eat as much as I wanted of whatever I wanted.

With only one short month to live, I would want to experience as much as I could, and this includes sex. Everything I had planned to do in the years after marriage would have to be done within the short time-frame I have left.

Before I die, I would know how sex feels. I would give my virginity to my special someone. I would know whether I liked it rough or gentle, slow or quick.

My one great regret would be not experiencing childbirth. Even if I could participate in the creation of a life, I could never raise my child. I could never see, hear, feel, or love the living extension of myself and my spouse, except in my dreams. ■

WHY IS YOUR BEST FRIEND YOUR BEST FRIEND?

PROMPT

If the World Were to End Tomorrow, What Would You Miss the Most?

I Am My Sister's Keeper

Cathleen Stone

Of course I would miss my family, my friends, my church, my school, and my whole lifestyle. But the thing I would miss the most would have to be my baby sister, Donae Stone, who is now 1 ½ years old.

Earlier in my sister's life, my family went through many changes and we were not able to see our father. During this time, I acted as a second parent while my mother worked to support us.

Eventually, my sister and I grew very close. After a while, we moved back with my father again.

Then Donae became sick with pneumonia. She became so sick that my family was afraid that she would die because at times her breathing was irregular and she stayed up late at night crying.

Many times, my mother was awake at night with my sister and I would assist by making bottles for her. I would also hold Donae and put her to sleep so that my mother would have a little peace. This was the time when we especially became close.

After what seemed like a very long time, Donae became well again. Thank God!

Another reason why I would miss Donae the most is because my aunts have babies. Sometimes I help them with their children. Looking at my aunt's babies made me want my mother to have another baby—one that I could help raise.

Donae fulfilled my wishes! Now each new event in Donae's life (for instance, her learning how to walk) is also an important event in my life. In the future, I want to have children of my own, but for now helping with Donae is enough.

Even though Donae is not perfect and annoys me sometimes, I will always love her. I would probably miss her the most if the world were to end tomorrow because she is a very important part of my life. ■

PROMPT

If You Could Be Anything in the World Besides a Human, What Would You Be? Why?

The Wind

Deeandra Leeshue

If I could be anything in the world, I'd want to be the wind. I would like to be the wind because I would be my own boss, blowing any way I feel like.

When I'm mad, I could spin fast to make a tornado, so that the world would know my rage. And on a hot summer day, I could blow a cool breeze, so I could watch kids come out and frolic.

I could bring lost loves back together, or choose to blow victim and murderer apart. I couldn't change minds but I could change lives. I could blow so cold, one could freeze to death. Or stop blowing, so windmills wouldn't work and farmers couldn't water their crops—nothing could grow and everyone would die.

I could blow just hard enough to help an old lady put her seeds in the ground and cover them with soil. When I bring them air and rain they'll grow beautifully, and she'll admire her garden happily every day.

Without me, birds couldn't find refuge in the sky or glide with the wind beneath their wings. I could pick the leaves up off the ground in autumn, and spin them so they create a beautiful show that people will have to stop and watch.

If I'm the wind, I'll have the power to create, destroy, and illuminate. ■

PROMPT

What Will Your Town or City Be Like in 50 Years?

Safe (?)

Emiley Prince-Barry

I walk the empty streets alone. In the darkness, the solar-powered lamps hesitate, giving light unwillingly. I encounter a computerized cop, asking for ID and time authorization. He confirms my documents. I walk on.

I go into an all-night coffee shop. The voice from the computer asks me to select. A doughnut with chocolate glaze pops up from inside the counter. All the while, I'm being scanned by the computer. I am allowed to leave.

I pass by some private houses. I notice the new bars put on the windows by the computers. A young boy looks out of the window at me as though he wishes he was me. His mother rushes him away from the window and sits him down in front of a computer.

Again I encounter a computerized cop. I show him the documents. As I wait for him to confirm them, I'm almost tempted to sneak a bite of my doughnut with chocolate glaze, but I remember that there's no eating on the sidewalk and I don't want to be trapped like most of the others.

In this neighborhood, I'm the only one who can enjoy the zero crime rate and the clean streets. I can also see the stars. I reach my destination: Central programming. I begin working on the program for tomorrow. ■

WHY IS YOUR BEST FRIEND YOUR BEST FRIEND?

> **PROMPT**
>
> What's One Change You Would Like to See in the Next Decade?

A Two-Day School Week

Amy Suen

My whole life, I have prayed for a two-day school week.

Every day I attend school from 7:30 in the morning until 2:25 in the afternoon. After school, I run to the subway station and hope I didn't miss the train to my job. After I get off from work, I go straight home and have my dinner. Then I get right to my house chores and homework.

It is really stressful and tiring for me to run from place to place. I have no choice but to cope because I know my education is very important for my future.

As for my job, it is also a necessity. My dad left our family when I was 7 years old and when my sister was 4. My mom tries really hard to support and raise us, but she can't do it on her own. She doesn't have the financial ability to raise us the way she wishes she could. Companies won't hire her because they say that she's too old and she doesn't know much English. So she went to apply for public assistance.

When I reached the age of 12, I started working for my uncle for a very low salary. But I did it anyway because I knew it would help my mom support the family.

Working and attending school at the same time is really hard. All the homework, tests, and projects just pile up like a stack of dirty clothes. It just never ends. Even if I've completed some of the projects, there's still more on the line.

I don't only work at my job, I also work at home. I have to tutor my sister, do house chores, and I have to do the cooking sometimes. By the time I arrive home from my job, I am already too tired even to have dinner. I just want to lie down on my bed.

Frequently, I forget to do some of my assignments, and the "wrong" way that I deal with it is to skip those classes because I am afraid that the teachers will scream their lungs out at me. At home I'm under so much pressure, fearing that the attendance office will call my house any minute to ask my mom the reason for my absence from classes.

I just wish school would be two days a week and the other five days could be a time for myself to do everything else. In the new decade, I really wish that school days could be shortened so my life wouldn't be so stressful. ■

PROMPT

If You Could Be a Member Of the Opposite Sex for One Day, What Would You Do? Why?

Whatever I Want

Jo Ann Gajadhar

If I were a member of the opposite sex for one day, I think I'd take full advantage of having more freedom and privileges. Boys get more because they are boys, and if I were a boy I'd take advantage of that.

I'd stay out late and play video games all day without having to worry about cleaning the house. And I'd also make a mess so that my little sister would have to clean it up.

My day as a guy would begin with me getting out of bed at 12 o'clock in the middle of the day. I'd force my little sister out of the bathroom, and then spend almost an hour there, knowing she has to use it because she has to go out. But I'd just stay in there listening to music and reading a magazine that I have no interest in, just to kill time.

I'd do all of this out of spite because I don't like my little sister. She acts like such a girl, listening to silly music every time I turn around. I get sick of listening to that corny music, so to get back at her I'll damage her CD while she's in the bathroom.

When she tells Mom what I've done, Mom won't believe her because Mom always believes me. I'm the older one. Then I'd play video games all day in my underwear. I'll leave such a mess out there that my little sister will have to clean it up when she comes home. She always has to clean up after me.

Then I'll intentionally spend an hour on the phone calling all those stupid sluts who gave me their numbers when I was at the club last night. Around 7 o'clock I'll get ready to go outside. I won't even have to ask because I know my parents will let me go. After all, I'm 17—I'm a man!

I'll go hang out with those crackheads that hang out in the building next to mine. At about 11 p.m., I'll leave them and go to the club and try to hook up with one of those sluts.

At about 4 o'clock, when I'm drunk and after I've fooled around with a couple of sluts, I'll go home and wake everybody up. I probably won't even make it to my room. I'll just pass out on the floor somewhere.

If I were a guy for one day, I'd spend it like that. Just to see how it feels, just for the experience. I don't actually agree with most of those things, but I'd do it regardless because guys get away with so much. And I just want to know for once in my life how it would feel to be carefree and be able to do whatever I want, whenever I want. ■

> **PROMPT**
>
> If You Could Have Any Super Power, What Would It Be and Why?

The Magical Touch

Sheneka Lewis

If I could have any super power, it would be the Magical Touch. I choose this because I would be able to help people who are sad, sick, or dead.

The Magical Touch could help people who are sad become happy again. By this I mean they would not forget what was bothering them, but they would be able to laugh once again. My Magical Touch would also be able to help people who are sick without a cure. I would help people with cancer, AIDS, etc.

The Magical Touch could also bring back life, but not all life. I couldn't bring back the life of someone who died years ago or more than 30 minutes ago. Bringing back someone who died years ago would not be a good thing. He might be so old that he's not used to the government we have or his family would not be the same as it was before he died. A lot of things could have changed since his death.

I also couldn't bring back the life of someone who died from a natural death. I think when a person dies naturally, God is calling them, so I would not be able to bring them back.

I'd only bring back the lives of people who died by accident. Accidental deaths, such as getting hit by a drunk driver, would cause a family more pain and suffering than if it was a natural death.

I don't want to be known just for my hand. I want to be known for helping people and their family and friends. The Magical Touch is a super power that can be used for anything, but I want to use it for the good and not the bad. Who knows, maybe my Magical Touch will bring world peace. ∎

WHY IS YOUR BEST FRIEND YOUR BEST FRIEND?

PROMPT

If You Could Direct a Music Video, What Would It Be Like? What Would You Put in It? Why?

Dancing in the Clouds

Venita Johnson

A young woman walks into a park with a host of trees and grass to her left. It's a pretty nice day outside, but partly cloudy. She is distressed.

She sits down and touches her arm and we flash back to when her boyfriend touched her arm. Then out of flashback, we see her touch her ring finger. We flash back to when he proposed to her and she fiddles with the ring. She smiles and the camera takes a close-up of his eyes. Now we switch to another memory. They're in a restaurant eating and someone walks in and starts shooting.

Then there's a collage of short, one-second scenes of how she and her boyfriend ducked under the table and then ran out the door and a short scene showing her expressions in the present day. Then, finally, as they're out the door, he gets shot, but you don't see him get shot. You only see the expression on her face, and then it fades into the present day scene.

She's crying now, until a ray of sunlight appears before her eyes. It beams on her tears and she looks up. The clouds are there. One is shaped like a ring and the other is shaped like a dancing crown for a queen. It excites her. Then she sees one that looks just like the boyfriend.

She runs towards it and then there's a flash of light and she's at an 18th century ball. Her boyfriend holds out his hand for a dance.

Imaginative Writing Prompts

She has on ballroom attire, and so does everyone else. They dance for a while, and after the dance is done, he takes her before the king and queen who are jolly and happy. He holds up her hand to show her ring and the king nods with his approval.

She's now in a bridal gown and he's in a groom's uniform. The preacher is about to start the ceremony. Then there's a rumbling underneath their feet and a trickle of water falls upon her head. Then there's a rainstorm falling on her. She lets go of his hand. The king points downward in a mean, angry way. She now throws herself in her boyfriend's arms (while she's disappearing), trying to hold on and kiss him once more.

Then you see an icy background and a girl spinning, which is meant to represent her falling back to earth. She looks like an ice queen. And we move back and forth between her disappearing and spinning back to earth until the second she kisses him, which is when she fully disappears. Her boyfriend closes his eyes and this ends the cloud scene.

Now all you see is the spinning ice queen and, for a few seconds, she'll slow down and look into the camera with her hand out. Then the camera focuses back on earth. The girl is trying to catch her breath. And she gets up and steps on the ring.

When she picks it up, she's happy and throws it up into the sky and runs in the opposite direction she came from, because now she's taking a new path in life. The end shot is of the ring being placed onto ice figures in cloudland. We have a close up of the ring and end the scene.

I chose this cloud idea because I have a fascination with clouds. They're so beautiful and look so full. I used to think that if you went up high enough, you could take a piece of it like cotton candy and put it in a jar on earth. But once I went on a plane, I realized I was going straight through a cloud and couldn't put it in a jar because it's made out of water vapor. But I still thought that they were beautiful to look at. ■

> **PROMPT**
>
> If You Could Create an Invention To Help Humanity, What Would It Be and What Would It Do?

Put Yourself in These Shoes

Eden Sidney Foster

If I were to invent something to help humanity, its function would be to enhance the presence of compassion in our lives. If we need anything, we need to be more humane.

Every one has heard the saying that warns us not to criticize a man until we've walked a mile in his shoes. If the human race took that advice to heart, we'd all be better off.

I'd invent a pair of shoes that would allow the wearer to empathize with another person at a higher level than we are capable of now. If a person could understand other people's lives as well as she does her own, there'd be less hatred, less ignorance, and less violence.

I imagine that if I wore this pair of shoes during a fight with a friend, I could truly see the situation through their eyes, and make a more informed, sensitive decision. I imagine that if politicians could wear these shoes and feel the pain of the people they're supposed to serve as acutely as they do their own, our country would be a happier, more united place. Assumptions and stereotypes would disappear and be replaced by truth.

I believe that promoting understanding is the only way to promote peace and creative change. Still, my magic shoes are only a fantasy.

Fortunately, reality provides things that may serve in their place. Art, theatre, writing, poetry, music, education, and all the other forms of communication that are available to us can aid in our understanding of each other. I can think of nothing that would help humanity more. ■

PROMPT
If I Ruled the World...

I'd Promote Peace, Decrease Poverty, and Stop Pollution

Fatema Akter

Everyone wants to rule the world. The irony, however, is that when they get that power, they tend to do the same things others have done that they said they didn't like. That is why I don't want to rule the world!

But if I had to, I'd ban the researching and use of nuclear weapons because most countries waste their wealth and squander their human and natural resources on making weapons. Weapons increase the chance of war among countries. Nuclear proliferation is a major problem. That level of power also kills the morality and values of people and makes them insensitive to the suffering of others.

I'd increase the power and budget of the United Nations because that's the major coalition of countries in the world. With that added authority, the United Nations could properly promote the welfare of its member states.

I'd increase development assistance to lesser-developed countries. For example, I'd absolve their foreign debt and encourage them to have family planning. Moreover, I'd fund micro credit systems for all, especially poor families.

Environmentally friendly projects would be started. I'd gather people and talk with them about stopping air, water, and noise pollution. I'd start special projects to actively reduce the greenhouse effect caused by auto emissions and the chopping down of forests.

I'd increase and encourage continued and expanded recycling. I'd support funding for the research of alternative energy sources, like solar energy and new nonpolluting fuel for cars—the type used in the new "clean air" New York City buses. I'd have bio-gas plants built because bio-gas not only keeps air clean, but also keeps water clean by using waste products to create energy.

I'd make laws about playing music too loudly because the sound creates sound pollution, and is harmful to people's ears.

And I'd redirect money from the military industrial complex. I'd make sure that it was used for creative and positive projects to benefit humanity and our precious environment.

My mother policy would be "mind your own business" all over the world. It will help every country to go their own way without interfering with the internal affairs of other nations. Other countries could not create any kind of force to use on other nations. There'd no longer be the word "war." That word would only be found in the dictionary and special historical museums.

Finally, I'd tell the world not to praise me, but just pray for me so that I could do what I should for the benefit of humanity. I'd pray to the Creator to give me the power to make the globe more comfortable and remove jealousy, terrorism, envy, and sadness from the world. ■

WHY IS YOUR BEST FRIEND YOUR BEST FRIEND?

> **PROMPT**
> What Place and Time
> Would You Travel Back To? Why?

Driving Him Crazy
With 'Weekend at Bernie's'

Joey Papperello

If I went back in time, I'd go back to the day before TV was invented, wherever TV happened to be invented. I'd then "invent" a TV (purchased at Wal-Mart the day before I traveled back, $52.50 after coupon and sales tax). A small 13" would do just fine. It's not like I'd have any competition yet, and I'd have the advantage of full color.

I'd also have to bring a VCR along, as naturally there weren't any TV stations around to prove that it worked. In addition, I'd bring along my trusted copy of "Weekend at Bernie's" on VHS, to show the world of yesteryear the wonderment that is madcap, over-the-top, buddy comedy.

I'd bring the set to the inventor Philo Farnsworth's house, plug it in, and proceed to blow his mind. I'd assume he'd have quite a few questions to ask me about my amazing invention that he was just on the brink of creating.

I'm sure he'd ask about the resistors, the transistors, the capacitors, in addition to the many other pieces of technical apparatus ending in the suffix "or." He'd tell me how he'd kill to know how I got the sound to sync with the video so perfectly, the brilliant color display, and how I "virtually eliminated the smell of burning rubber!" But most of all, he'd ask how in the world they got Bernie to look so alive.

You might be wondering why I'd choose to go back to this specific time and place. Fame? Glory? The fact that, according to my father, everything back then, no matter what it was, cost a nickel?

These are all minuscule in comparison to the simple look of utter confusion and despair on the original inventor's face when he sees the world's first TV... I'm sorry, not TV, "The Watcho-Viewo-tron." ■

PROMPT

What Would You Do if You Could Make Yourself Invisible? Explain.

An Angel Out for Revenge

Rosemary Mendoza

If I had the gift of invisibility for a lifetime, I'd plan my adventures one step at a time. But if I had it temporarily, I would use it wisely and have fun with it to change something I dislike in people, including my family, and maybe even society.

First of all, I'd wake up in the morning, become invisible and scare my big sister, who likes to scare me. I'd jump up and down on her bed and start whispering in her ear, and then I'd pull her bedsheet off her. I'd probably leave her alone after she started crying and screaming like the maniac she is.

I wouldn't reveal myself to her. That's the condition of having my power: I could not expose myself to anyone or else I would lose my power of invisibility.

After that, I'd bother my aunt Zoë, and make her think she's gone insane by moving objects from one place to another, tangling her hair, pinching her and then screaming in her ear. Then I'd carry my little sister, Hillary, so that she'd think she could fly. I'd carry her to my cousin's room so that he'd get scared of her and finally stop bugging her.

Then I'd make my entrance into my parents' room, whispering in their ears that I'm a messenger from God telling them that Rosemary is an angel sent from Heaven to guard and protect them and that she deserves the best treatment from everyone and if she doesn't get it, then God will become upset with them.

I'd listen to their conversations only if they were interesting, like where they keep the candy in the house, or what they think of their daughters. Maybe I'd scare them a bit by moving things around, turning the air conditioner on and off and removing the bedsheets from them.

After I finish with the people in my house, I'd go upstairs and bother my uncle and his family, especially his wife. I'd whisper in her ear that she has to stop spreading gossip or else she'll be severely punished. Then I'd bother my 3-year-old cousin who is such a little brat, by mocking him and then turning invisible so that his parents would think he's gone crazy. I'd carry my newborn cousin around his house and play with him—during my invisibility, of course—so his mother would get scared.

I'd go to my friend Cristina's house and listen to her conversations. I'd write things in her mirror with red lipstick, and see that scared look in her face, which she so often tries to hide. She seems to be fearless, and I'd love to see her face once she realizes that she, like the rest of us, gets scared at times.

Then I'd go to Madison Square Garden when my favorite band is performing. I'd turn invisible so that I could get in for free. I'd go backstage and maybe even to their dressing rooms. Then I'd become visible and tell them I was a reporter and that I'd like to interview them. I'd get their autographs and convince them to perform in my school. I'd then turn invisible and bother them for a bit just to see if they get scared easily.

I'd walk into a fancy restaurant where I'd see the president and the mayor eating, and I'd bother them. I'd pull their hair and tie their shoelaces together so that when they stood up, they'd trip and fall in front of everyone. I'd write things on their napkins and tickle them. On the way back home, I'd stop by every restaurant and bakery in sight, and eat as much as I could. I'd take the train and bother the people there by switching the lights off and on, pulling people's hair and making lots of noise.

I'd be fatigued after my adventure had ended for the day. I'd think about all the things I did and feel bad because I wouldn't like someone doing those sorts of things to me. I'd be very sorry, but I would still reminisce and laugh at everything I did. I'd walk into my house and act as if nothing happened, telling my family I went to a friend's house for the day to work on a project. They'd all look very insane and confused by everything that happened, but I still wouldn't crack and tell them, for I wouldn't want to lose this gift. I'd feel very giddy about what my next adventure would be. ∎

Imaginative Writing Prompts

PROMPT

If You Could Live in a Book, Movie, or TV Show, What Would It Be and Why?

I'm in 7th Heaven

Katelyn Baum

I wish that I could live like the characters in the old TV show "7th Heaven." When first watching the show, I didn't like it much. The family, the Camdens, seemed too unreal. They live in a big house and the father is a minister. The mother stays at home and takes care of the five kids and the dog.

Here I am, a 17-year-old teen mom living in a group home. I thought, "Who lives their lives like that?" But I gave the show a chance and kept watching it.

I realize now that "7th Heaven" isn't all sweet and dandy. They show realistic things that happen every day, like drugs, death, and teen pregnancy.

At the end of each show, the family seems to overcome their problems and still be together as a whole. I look at my life now and can relate to the show.

In "7th Heaven" the family is big—lots of kids, things going on all the time, some good, some bad. In my group home—with six moms, six children—it's like a big family, too. We all go through a lot.

Some people I know ask me why I watch the show. They tell me that the show is dumb. "I don't think so," I tell them. I know not everybody's life is like that, with two loving parents, siblings who care and look out for each other, and a nice house. But people still wish they could live like that.

After every show, I sit and think about how my life would be as one of the kids in the Camden family, and how nice it would be, and how loved I would be. ■

Imaginative Writing Prompts

PROMPT

If You Could Invent Something, What Would It Be? How Would It Work?

See Your Dreams on Tape

Emilio Rodriguez

Have you ever tried to tell a dream to your friends, but found you couldn't remember the whole dream? Then, as you tell bits and pieces of your dream, you find that it makes no sense? Well, ladies and gentlemen, I have the answer to this problem.

Introducing the Dream-O Digital Recorder! Dream-O is a device that records your dreams as you sleep. Now when you wake up, you can tell your friends your whole dream. You'll never again have to worry, "What did I dream about?" Now you can finally figure out what your dreams might be trying to tell you.

Throughout life, I've had some interesting dreams that I've wanted to tell people, but I can't remember many details. With a Dream-O Digital Recorder this problem will occur no more.

When you sleep at night, you put on the Dream-O comfortable head covering, which comes in a variety of colors and sizes. You plug the spiral cord into the Dream-O Digital Recorder. You insert your Dream-O videotape into the recorder, and press record. The Dream-O videotape can record up to 10 hours of dreams.

Now you can lie back and dream away. When you wake up in the morning, eject your Dream-O videotape and insert it into your VCR. Then you can watch your dream and tell your friends all about it, or let them sit back and enjoy watching it in the comfort of your home.

WHY IS YOUR BEST FRIEND YOUR BEST FRIEND?

Dream-O's comfortable head covering has two small disks. These disks are the digital transmitters. While the disks are smoothly massaging your head as you sleep, they are also recording your dreams. These disks read your brain waves, transform them into microwaves, and digitally record whatever you see in your dreams.

Have fun with your dreams. Compare a week's worth of dreams and see if they're connected. Compare your dreams to your friends' dreams. Are your friends in your dreams? Show them what they did. This is the beauty of Dream-O's Digital Recorder.

And Dream-O has a lot more to offer than just the machine. We're having a nationwide contest for the world's best dream! Does your dream have what it takes to be the best? Find out by owning your own Dream-O Digital Recorder. Submit your dream with the form you find in every Dream-O Digital Recorder box.

Stop wasting your imagination and forgetting your dreams. Get your Dream-O today. Or get left in La La Land. ■

Guide to Essays

INDEX BY TOPIC/THEME

African-American Youth
If You Could Change Your Race,
  Would You? 47
Bad Hair Days 72
A Double Life? 141

Arab Youth
Describe Your Ideal Mate 37
Who Are You More Comfortable
  With—Your Friends or Your
  Family? Explain. 61

Boyfriend/Girlfriend
Describe Your Ideal Mate 37
Have You Ever Cheated on Your
  Boyfriend or Girlfriend? 49
Describe Your First Love.....................65
What's the Most Unusual or Dramatic
  Thing You've Done (or Can Imagine
  Doing) to Convince Someone to Go
  Out with You? 77
How Was Your First Kiss, or How
  Would You Want It to Be? 81
What Should Teens Know or Do
  Before Having Sex? 116

Bullies
What's the Hardest Thing You've Ever
  Had to Do?......................................91

Community Issues
If You Could Solve One Problem
  Facing Teenagers, What Would It Be
  and How Would You Solve It? 115
If You Had Supernatural Powers,
  What Would You Do? 123
If You Could Have Someone Be Your
  Personal Slave for a Day, Who
  Would It Be? 140
What Will Your Town or City Be Like
  in 50 Years? 149
If I Ruled the World…......................160

Consumerism/Money
Love or Money?...................................70
What Brings Out the Beast in You?,
131

Disabilities
What Stereotypes Do You Think
  People Have of You That You
  Would Like to
  Change? Why? 46
What's a Mistake That You've Made
  That You Don't Regret? Explain.....99

173

Guide to Writing Prompts

Domestic Violence
Write a Letter to Your Parents, Telling Them What's Going On in Your Life That They Should Know About—but Don't 110

Drugs
Should Marijuana Be Legalized? 118

English Language Learners (ELL)
What's the Hardest Thing You've Ever Had to Do? 91

Family/Family Relations
How Would You Describe Your Family? 32
If One or Both of Your Parents Deserted You and Then Came Back Years Later Wanting to Know You, How Would You Handle It? 39
If You Could Switch Places with Anyone, Who Would it Be? 57
What is the Most Spiteful Thing You've Done or Had Done to You? How Did It Make You Feel, and Why? 89
What Would a Movie of Your Life Be About, and Who Would Play You? 96
What's Your Most Memorable Summer Experience? 104
If You Had $10,000 and Only a Day to Spend It, What Would You Spend It On? 135
If the World Were to End Tomorrow, What Would You Miss the Most? 146
What Would You Do If You Could Make Yourself Invisible? 164

Fathers
If You Could Switch Places with Anyone, Who Would it Be? 57
What Song or Movie Best Reflects Your Life, and Why? 87

Describe Your Best or Worst Holiday Memory 94
What Would a Movie of Your Life Be About, and Who Would Play You? 96

Foster Care
If One or Both of Your Parents Deserted You and Then Came Back Years Later Wanting to Know You, How Would You Handle It? 39

Friendship
Why Is Your Best Friend Your Best Friend? 31
Have You Ever Betrayed or Been Betrayed by a Friend? Explain 59
What Is Your Biggest Regret? 82
What's a Mistake That You've Made That You Don't Regret? Explain. ... 99

Humiliation
Bad Hair Days, 72
What Is the Most Embarrassing Thing You've Ever Done and Why? 86
What's a Mistake That You've Made That You Don't Regret? Explain. ... 99
What Is the Funniest Thing That's Ever Happened to You? 108

Identity
Bad Hair Days 72
What's Something You Hide From People That You Secretly Want Them to Know? Explain. 102

Jewish Youth
Who Are You More Comfortable With—Your Friends or Your Family? Explain 61

Latino Youth
Many of the authors are Latino youth

Guide to Writing Prompts

Loss/Bereavement
If You Could Rid Yourself of Any Emotion, What Would It Be and Why?..53
When Was the Last Time You Cried and Why?..79
If You Could Go Back in Time and Change an Event In Your Life, What Would It Be? Why?........................106
What Happens After We Die?..........124

Regret
What Is Your Biggest Regret?.............82
If You Could Go Back in Time and Change an Event In Your Life, What Would It Be? Why?..............106

Screenplay
What Would a Movie of Your Life Be About, and Who Would Play You?..96
If You Could Direct a Music Video, What Would It Be Like? What Would You Put in It? Why?.........156

Sex/Sexuality/Gender issues
What Makes You Angry? And What Do You Do About It?........................51
Who Are Better—Men or Women? ...41
What's Something You Hide From People That You Secretly Want Them to Know? Explain.................102
What Should Teens Know or Do Before Having Sex? 116

Stereotypes
What Stereotypes Do You Think People Have of You That You Would Like to Change? Why?.......46

Stress
What's One Change You Would Like to See in the Next Decade?...........150

Summer Vacation
What's Your Most Memorable Summer Experience?.....................................104

Teachers
If You Could Give Your Teachers Grades. 43
Who's Your Most Memorable Teacher? Why Does He or She Stand Out?..55
Describe Something One of Your Teachers Has Done That's Had a Big Effect on You 74

Television
If You Could Live in a Book, Movie, or TV Show, What Would It Be and Why?...167

Violence
What's the Scariest Thing that Ever Happened to You?...........................68
What's the One Thing You've Done in Your Life That You're Most Proud of and Why?..76

INDEX BY GENRE/STYLE

Descriptive Writing
How Would You Describe Your Family?..32
How Is the World Going to End?....125

Dialect
Say It in Slang: If I Ruled the World..130

Humor
Bad Hair Days 72
What Was the Weirdest Dream You Ever Had? 128
If You Could Adopt a Wild Animal, What Would It Be? 144
If You Could Be a Member of the Opposite Sex For One Day, What Would You Do? Why?...................152

175

Guide to Writing Prompts

What Place and Time Would You Travel Back to? Why?......162
What Would You Do If You Could Make Yourself Invisible?......164
If You Could Invent Something, What Would It Be? How Would It Work?......169

Persuasive Essay
If You Could Solve One Problem Facing Teenagers, What Would It Be and How Would You Solve It?, 115
Should Marijuana Be Legalized?, 118

Poems
Write a Valentine to That Special Someone......35
What Is Your Biggest Regret?......82
Describe the Night Time Through the Eyes of a 5-Year-Old......138

Reminiscence
—of An Event
Have You Ever Betrayed or Been Betrayed by a Friend? Explain......59

What's the Scariest Thing that Ever Happened to You?......68
Bad Hair Days......72
When Was the Last Time You Cried and Why?......79
Describe Your Best or Worst Holiday Memory......94
What's a Mistake That You've Made That You Don't Regret? Explain.....99

—of Family Life
If One or Both of Your Parents Deserted You and Then Came Back Years Later Wanting to Know You, How Would You Handle It?......39

—of a Person
Describe Your Ideal Mate......37
What Is Your Biggest Regret?......82
If You Were to Die Today, What Would Your Friends and Family Say About You at Your Funeral?......86
What Song or Movie Best Reflects Your Life, and Why?, 87

—of a Place
What's the Greatest Natural High You've Ever Experienced?......66

—of School
Who's Your Most Memorable Teacher? Why Does He or She Stand Out?......55
Describe Something One of Your Teachers Has Done That's Had a Big Effect on You......74
What's the Hardest Thing You've Ever Had to Do? Explain.......91

About Youth Communication

Youth Communication, founded in 1980, is a nonprofit youth development program located in New York City whose mission is to teach writing, journalism, and leadership skills. The teenagers we train become writers for our websites and books and for two print magazines: *New Youth Connections,* a general-interest youth magazine, and *Represent,* a magazine by and for young people in foster care.

Each year, up to 100 young people participate in Youth Communication's school-year and summer journalism workshops, where they work under the direction of full-time professional editors. Most are African-American, Latino, or Asian, and many are recent immigrants. The opportunity to reach their peers with accurate portrayals of their lives and important self-help information motivates the young writers to create powerful stories.

Our goal is to run a strong youth development program in which teens produce high quality stories that inform and inspire their peers. Doing so requires us to be sensitive to the complicated lives and emotions of the teen participants while also providing an intellectually rigorous experience. We achieve that goal in the writing/teaching/editing relationship, which is the core of our program.

Our teaching and editorial process begins with discussions between adult editors and the teen staff. In those meetings, the teens and the editors work together to identify the most important issues in the teens' lives and to figure out how those issues can be turned into stories that will resonate with teen readers.

Once story topics are chosen, students begin the process of crafting their stories. For a personal story, that means revisiting events in one's past to understand their significance for the future. For a commentary, it means developing a logical and persuasive point of view. For a reported story, it means gathering information through research and interviews. Students look inward and outward as they try to make sense of their experiences and the world around them and find the points of intersection between personal and social concerns. That process can take a few weeks or a few months. Stories frequently go through ten or more drafts as students work under the guidance of their editors, the way any professional writer does.

Many of the students who walk through our doors have uneven skills, as a result of poor education, living under extremely stressful conditions, or coming from homes where English is a second language. Yet, to complete their stories, students must successfully perform a wide range of activities, including writing and rewriting, reading, discussion, reflection, research, interviewing, and typing. They must work as members of a team and they must accept individual responsibility. They learn to provide constructive criticism, and to accept it. They engage in explorations of truthfulness, fairness, and accuracy. They meet deadlines. They must develop the audacity to believe that they have something important to say and the humility to recognize that saying it well is not a process of instant gratification. Rather, it usually requires a long, hard struggle through many discussions and much rewriting.

It would be impossible to teach these skills and dispositions as separate, disconnected topics, like grammar, ethics, or assertiveness. However, we find that students make rapid progress when they are learning skills in the context of an inquiry that is personally significant to them and that will benefit their peers.

When teens publish their stories—in *New Youth Connections* and

About Youth Communication

Represent, on the web, and in other publications—they reach tens of thousands of teen and adult readers. Teachers, counselors, social workers, and other adults circulate the stories to young people in their classes and out-of-school youth programs. Adults tell us that teens in their programs—including many who are ordinarily resistant to reading—clamor for the stories. Teen readers report that the stories give them information they can't get anywhere else, and inspire them to reflect on their lives and open lines of communication with adults.

Writers usually participate in our program for one semester, though some stay much longer. Years later, many of them report that working here was a turning point in their lives—that it helped them acquire the confidence and skills that they needed for success in college and careers. Scores of our graduates have overcome tremendous obstacles to become journalists, writers, and novelists. They include National Book Award finalist and MacArthur Fellowship winner Edwidge Danticat, novelist Ernesto Quinonez, writer Veronica Chambers, and *New York Times* reporter Rachel Swarns. Hundreds more are working in law, business, and other careers. Many are teachers, principals, and youth workers, and several have started nonprofit youth programs themselves and work as mentors—helping another generation of young people develop their skills and find their voices.

Youth Communication is a nonprofit educational corporation. Contributions are gratefully accepted and are tax deductible to the fullest extent of the law.

To make a contribution, or for information about our publications and programs, including our catalog of over 100 books and curricula for hard-to-reach teens, see www.youthcomm.org

About the Editor

Al Desetta has been an editor of Youth Communication's two teen magazines, *Foster Care Youth United* (now known as *Represent*) and *New Youth Connections*. He was also an instructor in Youth Communication's juvenile prison writing program. In 1991, he became the organization's first director of teacher development, working with high school teachers to help them produce better writers and student publications.

Prior to working at Youth Communication, Desetta directed environmental education projects in New York City public high schools and worked as a reporter.

He has a master's degree in English literature from City College of the City University of New York and a bachelor's degree from the State University of New York at Binghamton, and he was a Revson Fellow at Columbia University for the 1990-91 academic year.

He is the editor of many books, including several other Youth Communication anthologies: *The Heart Knows Something Different: Teenage Voices from the Foster Care System*, *The Struggle to Be Strong*, and *The Courage to Be Yourself*. He is currently a freelance editor.

More Helpful Books From Youth Communication

The Struggle to Be Strong: True Stories by Teens About Overcoming Tough Times. Foreword by Veronica Chambers. Help young people identify and build on their own strengths with 30 personal stories about resiliency. (Free Spirit)

Starting With "I": Personal Stories by Teenagers. "Who am I and who do I want to become?" Thirty-five stories examine this question through the lens of race, ethnicity, gender, sexuality, family, and more. Increase this book's value with the free Teacher's Guide, available from youthcomm.org. (Youth Communication)

Real Stories, Real Teens. Inspire teens to read and recognize their strengths with this collection of 26 true stories by teens. The young writers describe how they overcame significant challenges and stayed true to themselves. Also includes the first chapters from three novels in the Bluford Series. (Youth Communication)

The Courage to Be Yourself: True Stories by Teens About Cliques, Conflicts, and Overcoming Peer Pressure. In 26 first-person stories, teens write about their lives with searing honesty. These stories will inspire young readers to reflect on their own lives, work through their problems, and help them discover who they really are. (Free Spirit)

Out With It: Gay and Straight Teens Write About Homosexuality. Break stereotypes and provide support with this unflinching look at gay life from a teen's perspective. With a focus on urban youth, this book also includes several heterosexual teens' transformative experiences with gay peers. (Youth Communication)

Things Get Hectic: Teens Write About the Violence That Surrounds Them. Violence is commonplace in many teens' lives, be it bullying, gangs, dating, or family relationships. Hear the experiences of victims, perpetrators, and witnesses through more than 50 real-world stories. (Youth Communication)

From Dropout to Achiever: Teens Write About School. Help teens overcome the challenges of graduating, which may involve overcoming family problems, bouncing back from a bad semester, or even dropping out for a time. These teens show how they achieve academic success. (Youth Communication)

My Secret Addiction: Teens Write About Cutting. These true accounts of cutting, or self-mutilation, offer a window into the personal and family situations that lead to this secret habit, and show how teens can get the help they need. (Youth Communication)

Sticks and Stones: Teens Write About Bullying. Shed light on bullying, as told from the perspectives of the bully, the victim, and the witness. These stories show why bullying occurs, the harm it causes, and how it might be prevented. (Youth Communication)

Boys to Men: Teens Write About Becoming a Man. The young men in this book write about confronting the challenges of growing up. Their honesty and courage make them role models for teens who are bombarded with contradictory messages about what it means to be a man. (Youth Communication)

Through Thick and Thin: Teens Write About Obesity, Eating Disorders, and Self Image. Help teens who struggle with obesity, eating disorders, and body weight issues. These stories show the pressures teens face when they are confronted by unrealistic standards for physical appearance, and how emotions can affect the way we eat. (Youth Communication)

To order these and other books, go to:
www.youthcomm.org
or call 212-279-0708 x115

www.ingramcontent.com/pod-product-compliance
Lightning Source LLC
Chambersburg PA
CBHW071712090426
42738CB00009B/1749